beyond
beading
basics

carole rodgers

kp

CINCINNATI, OHIO
mycraftivity.com

 Published by Krause Publications, an imprint of F+W Media, Inc., 4700 East Galbraith Road, Cincinnati, Ohio, 45236. (800) 289-0963. First Edition.

13 12 11 10 09   5 4 3 2 1

DISTRIBUTED IN CANADA BY FRASER DIRECT
100 Armstrong Avenue
Georgetown, ON, Canada L7G 5S4
Tel: (905) 877-4411

DISTRIBUTED IN THE U.K. AND EUROPE BY DAVID & CHARLES
Brunel House, Newton Abbot, Devon, TQ12 4PU, England
Tel: (+44) 1626 323200, Fax: (+44) 1626 323319
E-mail: postmaster@davidandcharles.co.uk

DISTRIBUTED IN AUSTRALIA BY CAPRICORN LINK
P.O. Box 704, S. Windsor NSW, 2756 Australia
Tel: (02) 4577-3555

Library of Congress Cataloging in Publication Data
Rodgers, Carole.
  Beyond beading basics / by Carole Rodgers. -- 1st ed.
    p. cm.
  Includes index.
  ISBN-13: 978-0-89689-925-4 (alk. paper)
  1. Beadwork. 2. Jewelry making. I. Title.
  TT860.R74 2009
  745.594'2--dc22   2009035455

Editors: Nancy Breen, Kristin Boys, Rachel Scheller
Designer: Michelle Thompson
Production coordinator: Greg Nock
Photographer: Richard Deliantoni
Stylists: Lauren Emmerling, Nora Martini

METRIC CONVERSION CHART

To convert	to	multiply by
Inches	Centimeters	2.54
Centimeters	Inches	0.4
Feet	Centimeters	30.5
Centimeters	Feet	0.03
Yards	Meters	0.9
Meters	Yards	1.1

dedication

For my sister, Gloria, who introduced me to beading and started me on my beading journey.

acknowledgments

I would like to express my sincere gratitude to some very talented and creative people who let me use their artwork to enhance the information in this book. Many also generously shared their knowledge of beading with me and you, the reader. Their names are included in the text and in *Resources* on page 140. Thank you, all.

I wish to thank the following companies for their help as well:

Beacon Adhesives
Beadalon
Christopher Neal, The World Round
Claspon-Claspoff
Jay's Indian Arts
Morning Light Emporium
Off Center productions
One-of-a-Kind Rock Shop/Designer Cabs
Star's Clasps
Tam Designs
Two Cranes
Wild Things Beads

Lastly, I wish to thank the people at Krause Publications for making this book happen: editor Nancy Breen, designer Michelle Thompson, photographer Richard Deliantoni and acquisitions editor Candy Wiza.

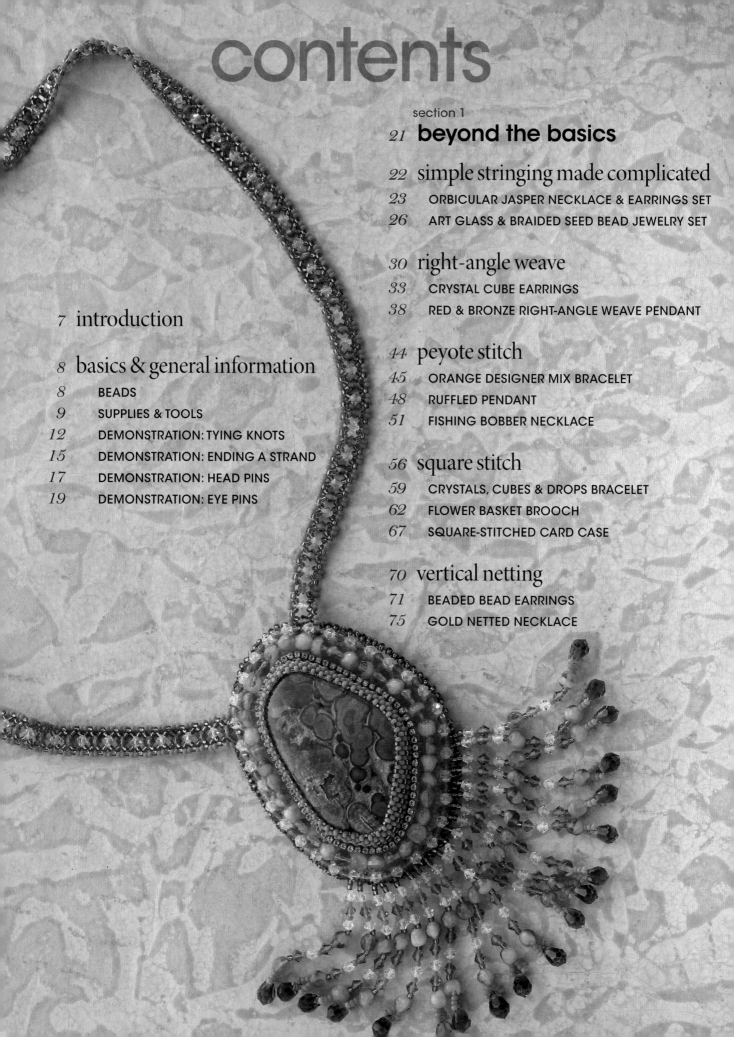

contents

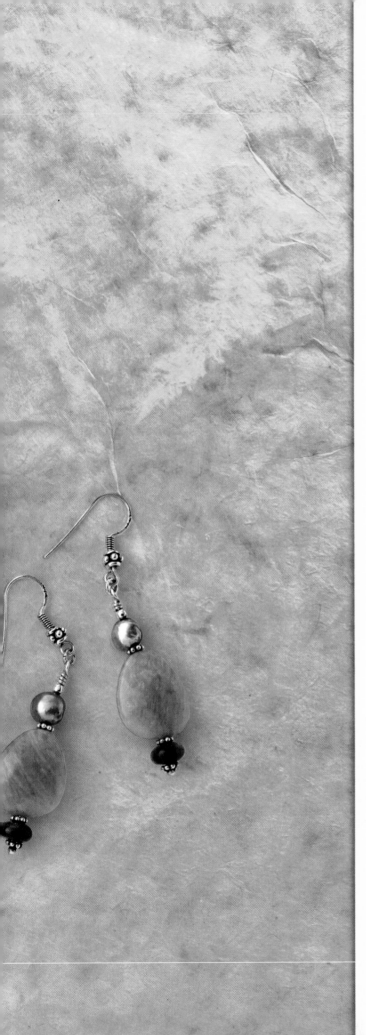

introduction

If you are looking for a greater beading challenge than simple stringing, then this book is for you. Instructions are included for doing several weaves I've developed over the years, as well as increasing and decreasing the basic weaving stitches I discussed in *Beading Basics* (Krause Publications, 2006), so you can learn to do more complicated projects. The various designs all use the techniques shown in the book. Many combine several of the techniques in one piece.

A friend told me recently that one of my best qualities as an artist/designer/author is that I "think outside the box" (or bead). You will find that many of these projects use common products in uncommon ways. I hope this gets you thinking about doing the same in your jewelry.

Don't limit yourself to just beads and findings or to following a pattern exactly as written. Look around your world and see what other things are out there that you can use for personal adornment and that you can include in your beading. Look for colors, textures and patterns that excite you. You can find inspiration in all sorts of places—even the hardware store on a boring trip to buy plumbing supplies. Just "think outside the bead or pattern" and see where it takes you.

I hope you find this book a useful friend and guide as you continue down the beading path. Have fun!

basics & general information

If you've been beading for a while, you've probably built up a stash of beads, needles and basic supplies. Most of those can be used in the projects in this book. There are a few projects that require unusual or harder-to-find beads and supplies; otherwise, every effort was made to use materials that you can easily obtain or make substitutions for.

This book is intended to be a guide that will get you to thinking of different ways to use products, weaves and your particular view of the world to make jewelry that reflects you and your style. The tips and techniques in this chapter are the methods I use when making jewelry. They are, by no means, the only ways to do things. If you have a method that works for you, use it. If you don't, try some of these. It never hurts to know more than one way to do something.

beads

You will need a variety of beads, including seed beads, pressed glass, metal and stone. In most cases, the size or shape of the bead is important to the project, not the material it's made from.

Since you may need to adjust the length or other aspects of the design in some projects, always allow for that and buy more beads than you think you will need.

Keep in mind that glass beads are manufactured in lots. Often, the color will vary from one lot to the next; it would be a disaster if you needed one or two beads to complete the design and the colors didn't match. Stone, wood and bone beads vary greatly in color and quality. Here, again, it is always wise to have more than you think you need.

Beads are usually sold and described by their measurements in millimeters. If a bead is described as an oval that is 9mm by 7mm, that means that the hole is 9mm long and the bead is 7mm wide. The hole length is usually given first. Of course, it's always smart to carry a bead gauge when buying beads so you can be certain. The tools are relatively inexpensive, and they take the guess work out of knowing sizes.

Seed beads are the exception to the above measuring system. A seed bead will be numbered with ° or /0 behind the number (6°, 8°, 11°, 15° or larger). The ° stands for *ought* and comes from an old way of numbering seed beads. Remember that the larger the number, the smaller the bead. A 6° seed bead is also known as an *E* bead.

BEAUTIFUL BEADS
The projects in this book use a variety of beads in different materials, colors and shapes.

supplies & tools

The following supplies and tools are necessary to have when you are ready to make that gorgeous creation. As with beads, when it comes to buying findings, threads and needles, try to have more on hand than you think you will need.

findings

Since you are ready for more advanced projects that require more time and effort than basic stringing, you might like to think about buying silver- or gold-plated findings if you don't already do that. Using an inferior clasp or findings on a spectacular piece of jewelry will seriously detract from the finished project.

Bead tips: The ones used here are the bottom hole clamshell tips that close around your knot to hide it from view. There is a diagram of the clamshell on page 16.

Clasps: The most commonly used clasps here are toggles, but a variety of decorative glass and metal buttons (for loop closures) will come in handy.

Crimp beads: These are used for ends of jewelry done on beading wire.

Earring findings: You can use whichever kind you prefer.

Eye pins: With eye pins, longer is always better. You can always cut them off, but it's impossible to add on to them. A minimum length of 2" (5cm) is suggested.

Head pins: See **Eye pins.**

Jump rings: Always have a variety of sizes and colors of jump rings.

Pin backs: The choice is up to you.

Split rings: As with the jump rings, you will need a variety of sizes and colors of split rings.

CLASPS

JUMP RINGS

SPLIT RINGS

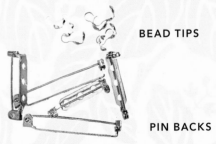

BEAD TIPS

PIN BACKS

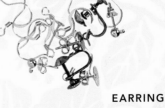

EARRING FINDINGS

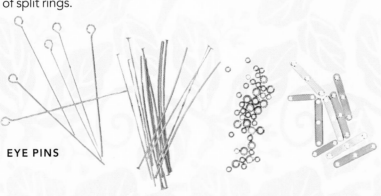

EYE PINS

HEAD PINS

CRIMP BEADS

CONNECTORS

needles

Beading: For most beading in this book, a size 10 or 12 beading needle will work. Have plenty on hand as they bend easily.

Sharps: These are short, sharp-pointed needles used for bead embroidery that are also useful for doing cabochon beading on leather. Again, size 10 or 12 is a good choice.

threads and stringing materials

Braided filament: Most of the projects here are done with braided filament line like FireLine™ Fishing Line, or WildFire™ and DandyLine™, which are actually made for beading. A variety of sizes were used depending on the strength needed. Both black and white are used as well. Be sure to use white with most crystals.

Silamide: This is a twisted nylon tailoring thread with a waxy feel that is widely used for bead weaving. It is very good for peyote and square stitch weaving.

Stringing wire: Braided strands of wire which are coated with plastic and come in a variety of strand numbers and weights.

glue

These are the glues used most often in the book. Other brands may be substituted. If a specific kind of glue is called for, like fabric glue, be sure to use that kind of glue for best results.

Fabri-Tac™: Used to attach leather to leather or fabric.

Gem-Tac™: Used for attaching stones and metal pieces to leather and other surfaces.

Super Glue: Used to attach metal pieces together.

BEADING NEEDLES

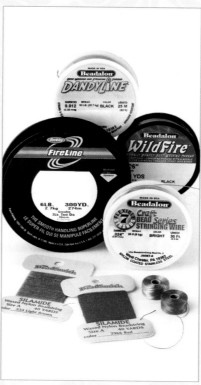

STRINGING MATERIALS

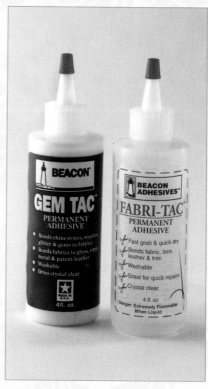

TYPES OF GLUE

tools

Bead gauge: This is a sliding ruler that allows you to accurately measure the size of beads in inches and millimeters. It is takes the guesswork out of sizing.

BEAD GAUGE

Bead sorting dish or cloth: Use your favorite method of sorting beads.

BEAD SORTING DISH

Chain nose pliers: These are pointed, smooth, flat jawed pliers.

CHAIN NOSE PLIERS

Crimp pliers: These are used for attaching and smoothing crimp beads.

CRIMP PLIERS

Needle nose pliers: These have a very pointed nose and are smooth jawed.

NEEDLE NOSE PLIERS

Round nose pliers: These have round, pointed noses.

ROUND NOSE PLIERS

Scissors: You will need two kinds of scissors—one for cutting thread and one for cutting braided filament, also known as *blade scissors.*

SCISSORS

Split ring pliers: These open the split ring so you can attach it to your work.

SPLIT RING PLIERS

Tool or storage box: You will need a place to keep it all together.

Wire cutters: You need a pair of wire cutters for cutting stringing wire and head/eye pins.

WIRE CUTTERS

Sooner or later, you are going to have to tie a knot in the middle of your beading. No one likes to do it. Knots make your work weaker. You have all those extra tail ends to work in. Tying knots is a pain!

There are, however, some knots that are easier to do and work better than other knots. My favorite is a weaver's knot. If you get proficient at using this knot, you can change threads in the middle of a project without it being noticeable. Here's how:

Weaver's Knot

A weaver's knot is a very effective way to join two threads together in the middle of a project.

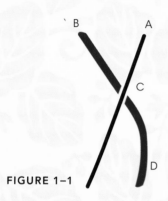

FIGURE 1–1

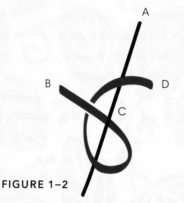

FIGURE 1–2

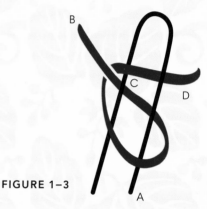

FIGURE 1–3

1 Refer to Figure 1–1: *A* is the end of the old thread and *B* is the end of the new thread. Cross them and hold between thumb and forefinger at point *C*. *D* is the new thread.

2 Pass *D* around and over *A*, up under *B* and over *A* again (Figure 1–2).

3 Then turn *A* down over *D*, over the new thread *B* and through the loop made by *D* (Figure 1–3).

4 Bring end *B* down and hold it with end *A*. Pull *D* tight, making sure you have pulled *A* down to where you want the knot. This knot slips through most seed beads and holds very well without being glued.

5 When you have tied on the new thread, weave the old ends back through the work, being sure to tie a half hitch knot after a few beads.

Half Hitch Knot

Half hitch knots are used most to weave in thread ends.

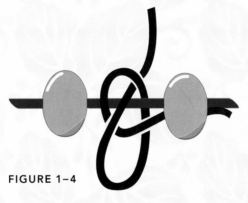

FIGURE 1–4

1 Take a small stitch over a thread between 2 beads in your work and pull the thread through until you have just a small loop of thread left.

2 Pass the needle through the loop (Figure 1–4) and pull tight.

3 Pass through a few beads and tie another half hitch knot.

4 Apply a very small amount of glue to the thread close to the knot and pass through a few more beads.

5 Pull the thread tight and cut off the excess close to a bead.

Square Knot

A square knot is good for ending threads, and it can be used to change threads in the middle of a piece.

FIGURE 1–5

FIGURE 1–6

1. Cross the thread in your right hand over the thread in your left hand, around and through to tie the knot (Figure 1–5).

2. Take the thread that's now in your left hand over the thread in your right hand, around and through to tie another knot (Figure 1–6).

3. Put a small amount of glue on the knot to make sure it stays secure.

Surgeon's Knot

1. To do a surgeon's knot, cross the right end of the thread over the left and pass through the loop.

2. Pass through again. Pull the ends to tighten.

FIGURE 1–7

3. Cross the left thread end over the right and pass through once. Tighten (Figure 1–7).

There are all sorts of ways to end a strand, but I find that the following methods work best for me.

Crimping

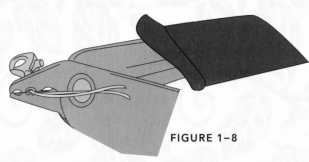

FIGURE 1–8

1 If you use bead wire for your strand, end that strand by threading on a crimp bead; then pass through your clasp or jump/split ring and back through the crimp bead into your bead strand. Be sure to pull the wire snug.

2 Using your crimp pliers in the *W* hole, bend the crimp bead tightly around the wire to secure (Figure 1–8).

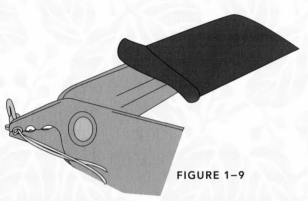

FIGURE 1–9

3 Put the crimped bead in the *O* hole of the pliers and press down and fold the bead over on itself to secure (Figure 1–9).

4 Work the wire through the beading for about ½" (13mm) and trim the end so it is hidden in the beads.

Using a Button

1 Make the closure an integral part of your beaded piece by attaching a large bead or button at the end of one strand.

2 Bead a loop big enough to go over the bead or button on the other end.

My Favorite Clamshell Method

1 Pass the thread through a crimp bead and tie several square knots around the crimp bead.

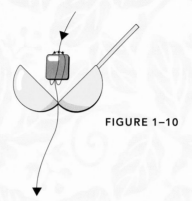

FIGURE 1–10

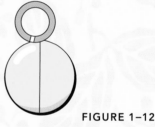

2 Take the thread through the bottom hole of the clamshell bead tip (Figure 1–10) to begin the necklace.

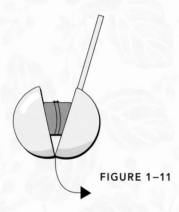

FIGURE 1–11

3 Glue the knots, trim the threads and close the clamshell around the crimp bead (Figure 1–11).

FIGURE 1–12

4 Bend the bar of the clamshell tip around in a loop (Figure 1–12).

Another Crimp Bead Option

1 When using heavier thread/bead wire, thread on a crimp bead before threading on the clamshell bead tip.

2 String on a second crimp bead.

3 Pass the thread/wire back through the clamshell tip hole, the first crimp bead and back through the beading.

4 Secure the crimp bead on the strand.

5 Trim the thread/wire ends.

6 Close the clamshell around the second crimp bead. This gives a nicer looking end to the thread.

There are two kinds of head pins—simple and wrapped. The simple pin has beads threaded on the shaft and a loop turned at the top to hold them and to allow you to hang the pin.

The wrapped pin has beads threaded on the shaft, but the loop is bent slightly above the beads. The tail of the pin is wrapped around the shaft, and the excess pin is cut off. These pins are secure. Your pin can't work off because there is no gap in the loop.

See my book *Beading Basics* (Krause Publications, 2006) for instructions on doing the simple pin, and follow the instructions below on how to construct a wrapped head pin.

Making a Wrapped Head Pin

1   Choose a pin that is 1" (25mm) to 1½" (4cm) longer than the length you need after you thread on your beads. Thread the beads onto the pin.

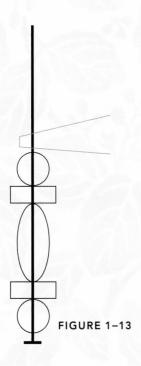

FIGURE 1–13

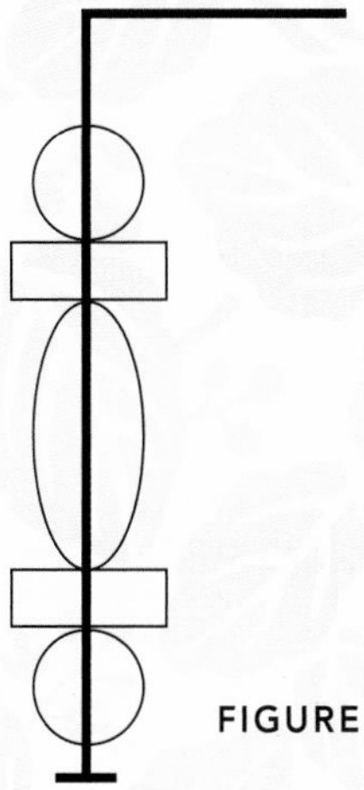

FIGURE 1–14

2   Grab the post of the pin with chain nose pliers just above the beads (Figure 1–13).

3   Bend the post in a right angle over the top of the pliers (Figure 1–14).

17

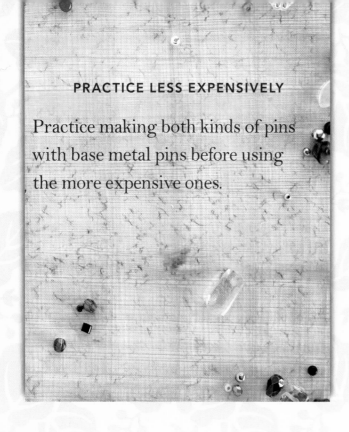

FIGURE 1–15

4. Change to round nose pliers. Place the ends as shown by the small circles in Figure 1–15. Grip the end of the pin with your fingers or chain nose pliers and wrap it around the upper pliers jaw.

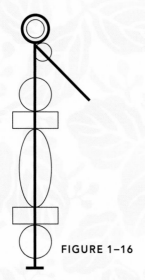

FIGURE 1–16

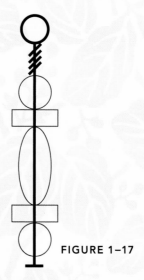

FIGURE 1–17

5. Continue around the jaw until you have made a full circle as shown in Figure 1–16.

6. Keep the round nose pliers in the loop. Hold the end of the pin with the chain nose pliers. Wrap the excess wire around the pin (Figure 1–17).

7. Trim excess wire with wire cutters close against the post. Work the wire end tight against the post with the chain nose pliers to keep from having a sharp point sticking out.

Eye pins are similar to head pins, but they have a loop on one end instead of a flat head. They are used to join two things together. Eye pins come in various lengths and materials just like head pins. The following instructions will show you how to use an eye pin.

Using an Eye Pin

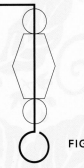

FIGURE 1–18

1 Thread beads on the eye pin. Trim the pin above the beads so you have 3/8" (9mm) left.

2 Use chain nose pliers to bend the end of the eye pin at a right angle to the body of the pin just above the beads (Figure 1–18). Be sure you bend the pin so it is lined up with the loop on the other end. If they aren't lined up, the pin will be twisted and will not work well.

FIGURE 1–19

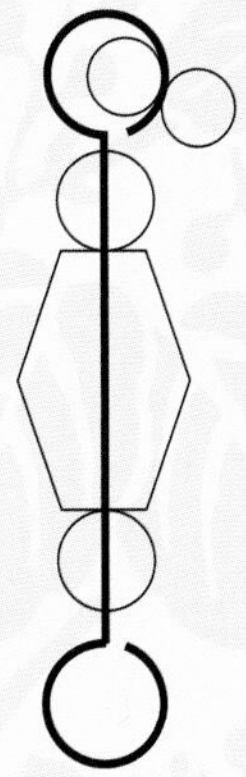

3 Grab the very end of the pin between the jaws of round nose pliers. While holding the pin with your other hand, curve the end of the pin around the nose of the pliers toward the bend to make a loop. (See Figure 1–19 and note the direction of the arrow.)

4 The pliers or pin will end up upside down. Be sure the loop is as tight against the pin as you can get it.

FIGURE 1–20

5 The finished pin should look like the one in Figure 1–20. If it is done correctly, it should lie flat on the table. Practice making pins before starting the project.

beyond the basics

Beading Basics (Krause Publications, 2006) provided you with all the basic knowledge you needed to make simple beaded jewelry. The purpose of this second book is to ratchet that knowledge up a peg or two. From learning ways to make a simple stringing project more complicated to picking up the rudiments of increasing and decreasing the basic stitches, you can further explore and experiment with new ways to expand your work in the projects that follow in this section. Once you learn to increase and decrease stitches, you can use those stitches to cover items with beads or make three-dimensional beaded projects. The possibilities are endless.

Each stitch has different uses, strengths and weaknesses. Right-angle weave makes a bead fabric that drapes well or structural pieces that maintain shape and rigidity depending on the beads and stringing materials used. Peyote is excellent for covering objects, making bags or just flat weaving. You can ruffle it or make it conform to a shape. Peyote is an extremely versatile stitch. Square stitch resembles loom weaving without all those warp threads to work in or having to work on a loom. It is an excellent stitch to use for doing pictures. Vertical netting is another stitch that makes a draping bead fabric. It is useful for covering items like vases and Christmas ornaments.

Experiment with the stitches. Try combining them or changing the sizes of beads in the same piece. Just play! You never know what you can do until you try.

Simple Stringing
Made Complicated

One of the easiest ways to make a simple stringing project more complicated is to add strands. If you want to take it further without getting into bead weaving, then try braiding. Even though these projects look nothing alike, they are each braided. The braids are done in different ways using different materials, but the basic method is the same.

The beading path has many twists and turns. Have fun figuring out which one you want to take.

1 stone pendant (Two Cranes, see *Resources*, page 140)

16 flat oval 12mm × 10mm stone beads (A)

16 faceted 20mm × 16mm triangular stone beads (B)

80 dark stone 4mm × 6mm rondelle beads (C)

96 light stone 4mm × 5mm beads (D)

82 irregular-shaped dyed 6mm pearls (E)

90 round 2.5mm silver beads (F)

10 grams size 13° silver Charlottes (G) (Wild Things Beads, see *Resources*, page 140)

32 Bali silver 4mm daisy spacers (H)

50 fluted round silver 4mm beads (I)

One 3 strand wide silver clasp (Claspon-Claspoff, see *Resources*, page 140)

1 pair silver ear wires

Two 2½" (6cm) silver head pins

Two 4mm silver jump rings

10 silver clamshell bead tips

Ten 2mm crimp beads

9 yards (8m) braided filament line 10lb. (DandyLine™ black .011" [.28mm] diameter)

2 size 10 beading needles

Blade scissors

Chain nose pliers

Round nose pliers

Bead sorting dish or cloth

Tape

orbicular jasper necklace & earrings set

There are a variety of types and sizes of stone in this necklace, and they work well together because the colors make a harmonious blend.

The pendant in this necklace came from Two Cranes. The strands accent the pendant and do not overpower it even though this is a heavy necklace. The thin strand of silver Charlottes adds the needed *pop* and accents the silver spacers used throughout. The instructions indicate the stone beads by shape, not name, as you probably will not find a piece just like this one.

Happy hunting for your treasure!

BEAD KEY

 12mm x 10mm flat oval (A)

 20mm x 16mm triangular (B)

 4mm x 6mm dark stone rondelle (C)

 4mm x 5mm light stone (D)

 6mm irregular pearl (E)

 2.5mm round silver (F)

 13° Charlottes (G)

 4mm Bali daisy spacer (H)

 4mm fluted round silver (I)

FIGURE 2–1

instructions

Note: *I refer to the beads by the abbreviations in the materials list and Bead Key (see Figure 2–1).*

The easiest way to make this necklace is from the center out in both directions. The finished length is 23" (58cm), but the strands are longer than that. If you wish to change the length, keep in mind that the necklace will shrink as you braid it.

making the first strand

1 Cut 2 yards (2m) of thread and double-thread 1 needle. Match ends, pass them through the 2nd needle and pull up so you have a few inches of thread hanging from the needle.

2 Always do the strand with the biggest beads first as it will be the one the others have to match for length. Pass 1 needle through the pendant and center on the thread. If the pendant hole is very large, thread on enough small round silver beads (F) to just fill the width of the hole.

3 On 1 side, begin threading on 1 Bali spacer (H), one 12mm × 10mm oval (A), 1 (H) and one 20mm × 16mm triangular (B). Repeat this pattern 6 more times for a total of 7 (B) beads.

4 End the strand on this side with 1 (H), 1 (A), 1 (H) and 1 (F). Tape the end to temporarily secure, or loop back through the (F) bead.

5 Repeat Steps 3 and 4 on the other side.

making the second strand

1 Cut 2 yards (2m) of thread and double-thread 1 needle. Match ends and pass them through the 2nd needle; pull up so you have a few inches of thread hanging from the needle.

2 If the hole still has room in it, thread on enough small round silver beads (F) to be as wide as the pendant. If not, pass through the hole and center the pendant on the thread.

3 On 1 needle, pick up one 4mm fluted silver bead (I) and two 4mm × 5mm light stone beads (D). Repeat till the strand is the same length as the 1st one. End with 1 (I) and 1 (F). Tape the end to temporarily secure, or loop back through the (F) bead.

4 Repeat Step 3 on the other side of the pendant.

making the third strand

1 For the 3rd strand, double-thread the needles as in Step 1, *Making the Second Strand.*

2 Use more small round beads if needed to pass through the hole. Center the pendant on the thread.

3 Alternately pick up 1 (F) and 1 dark stone bead (C) until you have the length you need. End with an (F) bead. Tape the strand.

4 Repeat for the other side.

24

making the fourth strand

1 Double-thread the needles and pass through the pendant, adding small beads if you need to in the hole.

2 On each side of the pendant, thread on enough pearls (E) to get the length you need.

3 Tape or tie off strands.

making the last strand

1 Cut 1 yard (1m) of thread and place a needle on each end.

2 Pass 1 needle through the pendant, adding Charlottes (G) if needed to finish filling up the hole.

3 Thread enough Charlottes (G) on each side of the pendant to get the length you need.

4 Tape or tie off the strands.

finishing the strands

1 Before braiding, separate the strands into 3 sets. Use the heaviest strand as 1 set, strands 2 and 5 as the 2nd set and the remaining 2 strands as the 3rd set.
Loosely braid the strands together on 1 side only. Check for length. Add or subtract beads as needed to get the lengths the same after braiding.

2 Pass the needle of 1 strand through a clamshell bead tip from the bottom. Remove the needle (cut the thread against the needle if it is the center of the thread, or simply remove it if it's the 2-thread needle).

3 Pass 1 thread through a crimp. Be sure the beads are pulled up snugly. Tie off the threads against the crimp as shown in *My Favorite Clamshell Method* on page 16.

4 Repeat Steps 2–3 for all remaining strands on that side.

5 Repeat Steps 1–4 for the other side.

attaching the clasp

1 The clasp has 3 loops on each side, and you have 5 strands. Two loops on each side will have 2 clamshells attached.

2 Work the ends around so that the pearl strand and the Charlotte strand both attach to an outside loop. Use the round nose pliers to bend the bars of the clamshell tips around the loop in the clasp. Repeat on the other side.

3 Attach the strand with the large beads in the center. Attach the remaining 2 strands to the 3rd loop on each side.

making the earrings

1 On 1 head pin, thread on 1 (H), 1 (C), 1 (H), 1 (B), 1 (H), 1 (E) and 1 (F).

2 Make a wrapped loop at the top of the pin (see *Making a Wrapped Pin* on page 17). Trim excess wire.

3 Attach the head pin to the ear wire with a jump ring.

4 Repeat Steps 1–3 for the other earring.

MATERIALS LIST

Two 2" (5cm) flat curved cane glass pieces in clear, copper, white and hot pink (David Christensen, see *Resources*, page 140)

17 bumpy copper large-holed 5.5mm × 8mm beads (A)

12 copper 4mm × 5.5mm spacer beads (B)

16 copper 4mm round fluted beads (C)

10 grams size 11° hot pink seed beads (D)

10 grams size 11° white luster seed beads (E)

10 grams size 11° copper-lined clear seed beads (F)

1 copper 18mm toggle clasp

1 pair copper ear wires

2 copper clamshell bead tips

4 copper crimp tubes

32 copper crimp beads

8 copper 4mm × 5mm jump rings

5 yards (5m) Beadalon® copper .015" (.38mm) diameter beading wire

Wire cutters

Crimping pliers

Chain nose pliers

Round nose pliers

Bead sorting dish or cloth

Tape

art glass & braided seed bead jewelry set

Seed beads are probably the most versatile bead you can buy. One lone bead may look insignificant, but when you see them used in mass, they can be very impressive.

While not *in mass*, the seeds used here combine to make a definite statement. The braiding is delicate, yet substantial. There is a secret to keeping it braided I share in the instructions.

This stringing project combines seed beads with larger metal beads and David Christensen cane glass pieces to make an unusual collar. You could use any kind of large focal pieces to create a similar look. Experiment and see what you can come up with.

FIGURE 2-2 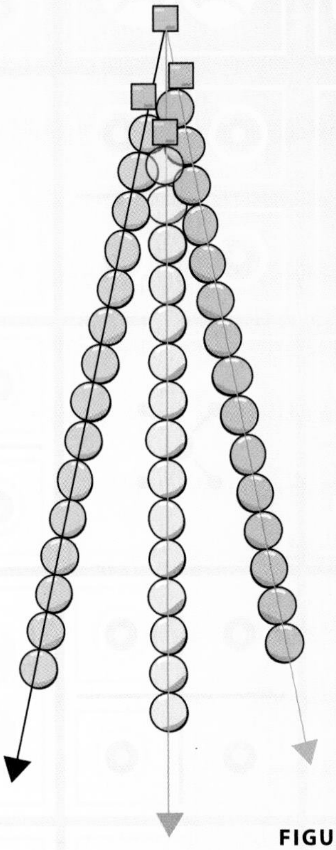   FIGURE 2-3    FIGURE 2-4

making the pendant

1 Cut 3 pieces of wire 1 yard (1m) long. Put 2 pieces aside.

2 On the 3rd strand, thread on 1 crimp and enough hot pink seeds (D) to make 3½" (9cm). Add a 2nd crimp. Center all.

3 Use the crimp pliers to smash the crimps tightly against the seeds on either side of the center of the strand (Figure 2–2).

4 Repeat Steps 2 and 3 using the white luster seeds (E) with the 2nd wire.

5 Repeat Steps 2 and 3 using the copper-lined clear seeds (F) with the 3rd wire.

6 When all 3 strands are threaded, place the ends together. Insert all 3 strands through another crimp, smashing it up tightly against the 3 crimps already there (Figure 2–3).

7 Loosely braid the strands together, matching crimps on the other end. Thread all 3 strands through a crimp and smash (Figure2–4).

making the necklace

1 Pass 1 set of 3 strands through a bumpy copper bead (A). Make a loop with the braided beads and pass the other set of ends through the (A) bead from the opposite direction, pulling up snug. Tape 1 set of ends to keep them from moving.

2 On the other set of ends, pick up 1 fluted round bead (C), 1 (A), 1 (C) and 1 copper spacer (B).

3 Pass through 1 cane glass piece.

4 Pick up 1 (B), 1 (C), 1 (A), 1 (C), 1 (A), 1 (C), 1 (A) and 1 (C).

5 Pass all strands through a crimp. Smash the crimp around the 3 wires.

6 On 1 wire, thread on 4" (10cm) of hot pink seeds (D) and 1 crimp. Push up tight and smash the crimp around the wire.

7 Repeat Step 6 on the 2nd wire with white luster seeds (E).

8 Repeat Step 6 on the 3rd wire with copper-lined clear seeds (F).

9 Braid the strands.

10 Pass all strands through a crimp. Smash the crimp around the strands.

11 Thread on 1 (A), 1 (C), 1 (A), 1 (C), 1 (A) and 3 (B).

12 Pass all wires through a crimp tube and loop the end of the toggle. Pass wires back through the crimp and into the beading for about ½" (13mm). Pull beads up snug. Smash the crimp tube and trim the wires.

13 Remove the tape from the other set of wires.

14 Repeat Steps 2–11.

15 Hook 3 jump rings together. To reinforce, add another jump ring to each link (see the photo above). Attach 1 end to the bar end of the toggle.

16 Pass the wires through a crimp tube, the end set of jump rings and back into the beading about ½" (13mm). Pull up snug.

17 Smash the crimp and trim the excess wires.

making the earrings

1 Cut three 12" (30cm) pieces of wire.

2 On each, thread on 3" (8cm) worth of seeds.

3 Center the beads on the wire

4 Place a crimp at each end and smash.

5 Pass all wires through 1 crimp and up tight against the beads. Smash the crimp.

6 Braid the seed strands.

7 Pass all wires through another crimp and smash in place.

8 Take all wires through 1 (A) and 1 (B).

9 Pass through the bottom of the clamshell bead tip.

10 Pass all wires through a crimp tube. Smash. Trim the wires. Close the clamshell.

11 Bend the bar of the clamshell into a loop. Attach the loop to an ear wire with a jump ring.

12 Repeat Steps 1–11 for the other earring.

WIRE-WRAPPED PENDANT

This piece of chrysocolla drusy was beautifully wire-wrapped by Deb Penrod of Designer Cabs. It's another example of how braiding multiple strands makes an elegant necklace.

Right-Angle Weave

Right-angle weave can be done with one needle or with two, although some call the double-needle version *cross weave*. Both look the same. Try both methods and choose the one you prefer. The double-needle method does work up much faster because you are passing through the beads fewer times.

Right-angle weave is composed of patterns of four beads. These patterns are called squares. If you use bugle beads or other straight beads, the pattern does make a square. If you use round or bicone beads, the pattern looks more like a diamond.

Right-angle weave does not work well with all beads. Bugles, rounds, ovals and bicones generally work the best. If you are unsure, experiment with your beads to see if they will work. How-tos for both methods of the basic weave follow in this chapter.

Double-Needle Right-Angle Weave

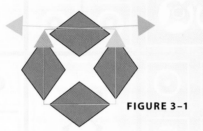

FIGURE 3–1

FIGURE 3–2

1 Place a needle on each end of the thread; be sure to keep the thread in the needles even in length.

2 String 4 beads on 1 needle and center them on the thread.

3 Insert the 2nd needle through the last bead you picked up, passing from the opposite direction, and pull up snug to form a square or diamond shape centered on the thread (Figure 3–1). You can use more than 1 bead per side, but the pattern in regular right-angle weave will always have 4 sides.

4 To continue, string 2 beads on the 1st needle and 1 bead on the 2nd needle, then pass the 2nd needle through the last bead on the 1st needle and pull up snug, creating 2 squares (Figure 3–2).

5 Continue in this manner until you have the desired length. You are continuously doing a figure-eight pattern with the 2 needles.

RIGHT-ANGLE BRACELETS WITH ART BEADS

These two bracelets are the same right-angle weave pattern using different beads. The horse head bead was done by Kathy Johnson and the denim bead by Theresa Provine.

Single-Needle Right-Angle Weave

1 Cut a length of thread and single-thread the needle.

2 String on 4 beads and tie them together in a square knot between beads 1 and 4, close to the end of the thread (Figure 3–3). Be careful not to tie them too tightly as you need a little wiggle room.

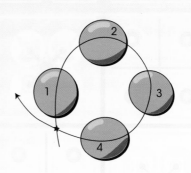

FIGURE 3–3

3 Pass the needle and thread back through beads 1, 2 and 3 (Figure 3–4).

4 String on 3 more beads (5, 6 and 7).

5 Pass back through bead 3 of the 1st square and then through beads 5 and 6 in the 2nd square (Figure 3–5).

6 String on 3 more beads (8, 9 and 10) and pass back through beads 6, 8 and 9 (Figure 3–6).

7 Continue picking up 3 beads for each new square until you have the desired length.

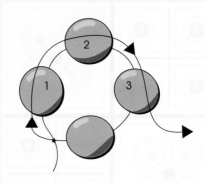

FIGURE 3–4

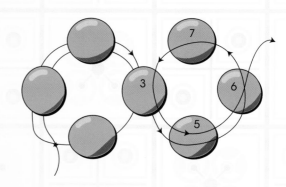

FIGURE 3–5

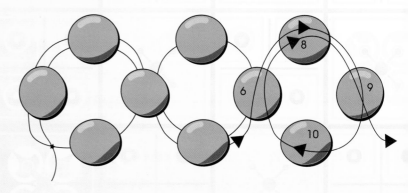

FIGURE 3–6

MATERIALS LIST

80 sapphire aurora borealis (AB) 4mm bicone crystals (A)

52 clear aurora borealis (AB) 4mm bicone crystals (B)

2 crystal aurora borealis (AB) 7mm × 6mm tear drops (C)

2 Bali silver 5mm daisy spacers (D)

2 decorative silver 3" (8cm) head pins

1 pair decorative Bali ear wires

1 spool 32 gauge brass wire

Wire cutters

Chain nose pliers

Round nose pliers

crystal cube earrings

These earrings provide a lesson on doing multiple rows of right-angle weave. These cubes look complicated, but actually they are a strip of right-angle weave folded into a box with the ends worked in. Be sure to do these in the two-needle method when working with wire.

Beads, wire and right-angle weave are an excellent combination. You can use wire the same as you do thread, but wire goes beyond what you can do with thread. Because wire is stiffer, you can create all sorts of structural projects, like these cube earrings.

BEAD KEY

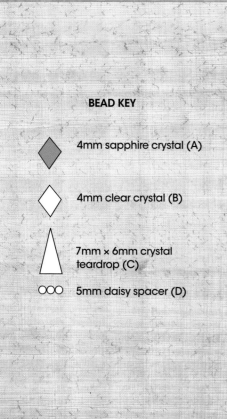

◆ 4mm sapphire crystal (A)

◇ 4mm clear crystal (B)

▲ 7mm × 6mm crystal teardrop (C)

∞ 5mm daisy spacer (D)

FIGURE 3–7

making the first row

1 Cut a piece of wire about 4' (122cm) long. If you're unfamiliar with working with wire, see *A Few Tips About Wire* on page 37 .

2 Thread on 4 sapphire crystals (A) and center them on the wire.

3 Refer to the basic instructions and Figure 3–1 on page 31.
Insert the 2nd wire through the last bead you picked up, passing from the opposite direction, and pull up snug to form a diamond shape, which should be centered on your wire.

4 Pick up 1 clear crystal (B) on the right-hand wire and 2 sapphire crystals (A) on the left-hand wire.

5 Pass the right-hand wire through the last sapphire bead you picked up and pull snug. (See Figure 3–2 on page 31.)

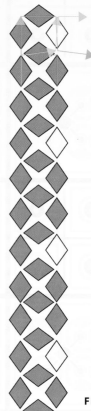

FIGURE 3–8

6 Continue adding beads as in Step 5, following the pattern in Figure 3–8 until you have completed 10 of the 11 squares in the band.

7 For the final square, pick up 2 sapphire beads (A) and 1 clear crystal (B) on the left-hand wire (Figure 3–8).

8 Pass the right-hand wire through the clear crystal (B) only and pull snug.

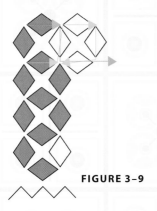

FIGURE 3-9

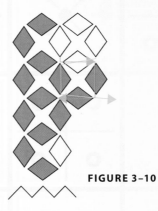

FIGURE 3-10

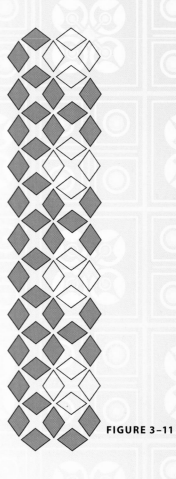

FIGURE 3-11

turning the corner for the second row

1 Your wires should be coming out of the side of the band facing away from the work (Figure 3–8, page 34).

2 To start the 2nd row, pick up 3 clear crystals on the top wire.

3 Pass the bottom wire through the last crystal (Figure 3–9).

4 Pass the inside wire (shown in Figure 3–10 in yellow) into the sapphire bead from the previous row.

5 On the other wire, pick up 2 sapphire beads. Pass the inside wire through the 2nd sapphire bead as shown. Pull snug.

6 Continue in this manner down the 2nd row, being sure to follow the pattern in Figure 3–11.

7 Turn the corner at the end of the row the same as you did at the top.

FIGURE 3-12

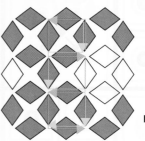

FIGURE 3-13

adding the last row

1 Begin the new row the same as you did on the 2nd row. All the beads in this row are sapphire.

2 Refer to Figure 3–12, the pattern showing the final row added. Follow it to the bottom. The wires should be coming out of the end bead of the row.

3 If you have to change wire during the weaving, work the ends around until they come out the same hole. Twist the ends together and trim the wire ends to about ½" (13mm). Roll the ends into a tiny ball so the points are not sticking out. Always end wires on the same side of the piece.

4 To add a wire, simply insert it where it should be, center and continue weaving.

joining the band

1 Roll the band so the narrow ends meet, being sure any wire joints are on the inside.

2 Pick up a sapphire bead on the wire closest to the end of the band.

3 Pass the wire into the vertical sapphire bead on the other end of the band (Figure 3–13).

4 Pick up a sapphire bead on either wire and pass the other through it from the opposite direction (Figure 3–13). Pull snug.

5 Continue down the piece as shown until you get to the end following the graphic.

6 Work wire ends around, twist together, trim and roll as above.

7 Refer to Figure 3–12, noting the orange lines. Carefully crease the band at each orange line marked so you make a 4-sided box.

Working with wire is relatively easy. Wire has memory. Because it comes coiled on a spool, it has a tendency to kink. Cut a piece of wire and run it gently through your fingers several times to smooth it. When you pull it through beads, do so slowly and watch to make sure it doesn't kink. If it does start to kink, back out, put your finger in the loop and pull it over your finger or something round like a pencil.

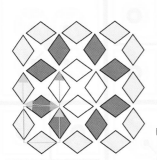

FIGURE 3–14

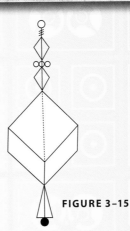

FIGURE 3–15

finishing the cube

1 Cut about 18" (46cm) of wire. Work the wire into 1 of the corner beads on 1 corner of the square you made. Center it. (Refer to Figure 3–14; the beads that form the band already woven are shown in gray.)

2 Refer to Figure 3–14. Pick up 2 sapphire beads on the right-hand wire.

3 Pass the left-hand wire through the 2nd bead and pull snug.

4 Pass the left-hand wire through the next bead on the existing band (shown in gray).

5 On the other wire, pick up 1 clear crystal and 1 sapphire bead.

6 Pass the left-hand wire through the sapphire bead.

7 Continue in this manner working up and down the rows until you fill up the side, being sure to follow the pattern as shown in the graphic.

8 Repeat Steps 1–7 for the other side.

9 Repeat all steps to make the 2nd cube.

assembling the earrings

1 Referring to Figure 3–15, thread 1 crystal teardrop (C) on the head pin, large side first.

2 Thread on 1 of the cubes diagonally through the corners.

3 Next add a clear crystal (B), 1 daisy spacer (D) and 1 clear crystal (B).

4 Finish the pin in a wrapped loop. See *Making a Wrapped Head Pin* on pages 17–18.

5 Carefully open the loop on the earring finding and insert the pin. Close.

6 Repeat Steps 1–4 for the other cube.

37

MATERIALS LIST

15 grams bronze 3mm
Japanese bugle beads

10 grams size 11°
red/bronze seed beads

121 red/bronze 4mm
fire polish beads

5 bronze 8mm fire
polish beads

15 bronze 3mm ×
16mm dagger beads

1 red/bronze 18mm
shank button

DandyLine™ .008"
(.2mm) diameter black
thread or 8lb. black
braided filament

2 size 10 or 12
beading needles

Blade scissors

Glue

Bead sorting
dish or cloth

red & bronze right-angle weave pendant

A piece of right-angle weave is an excellent canvas for embellishment. It is easy to add surface decoration to enhance the look and make the piece richer and more in-depth. The descending and ascending rows of this piece will teach you how to decrease and increase the stitch to veer away from the basic rectangular or square shape usually associated with the weave.

Use Japanese bugle beads for this project. They have smoother shoulders and won't fray your thread as badly.

The instructions are given for the double-needle right-angle weave, but this one you can do with one needle. Follow the pattern and make this piece as shown, or choose which areas you want to embellish and make it your own. Only five different beads were used, so colors can be easily changed to suit your taste.

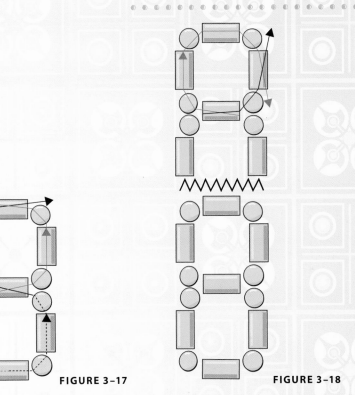

FIGURE 3–16   FIGURE 3–17   FIGURE 3–18

weaving the center row

1 Cut a 2 yard (2m) length of thread (or more, if you can handle it) and place a needle on each end. Pull up thread ends so they are even in length.

2 Refer to Figure 3–16 and pick up 1 seed, 1 bugle, 1 seed, 1 bugle, 1 seed, 1 bugle, 1 seed and 1 bugle.

3 Center the beads on your thread. From the opposite directon, pass the 2nd needle through the last bugle and pull up snug (Figure 3–16), making a square.

4 On 1 needle, pick up 1 seed, 1 bugle, 1 seed and 1 bugle.

5 Using the 2nd needle, pick up 1 seed, 1 bugle and 1 seed.

6 From the opposite direction, pass the 2nd needle through the last bugle you picked up on the 1st needle and pull snug—you now have 2 squares (Figure 3–17).

7 Continue repeating Steps 4–6 until you have 8 squares completed.

8 For the ninth square, refer to Figure 3–18. On the left-hand needle, pick up 1 seed, 1 bugle, 1 seed, 1 bugle and 1 seed.

9 On the right-hand needle (as you look at the diagram), pick up 1 seed and 1 bugle.

10 From the opposite direction, pass the left-hand needle through the right-hand bugle and pull up snug (Figure 3–18). The threads should be coming out of the side of the square as shown.

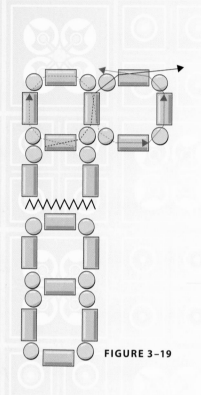

FIGURE 3–19

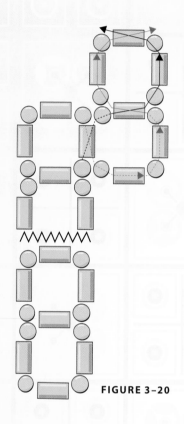

FIGURE 3–20

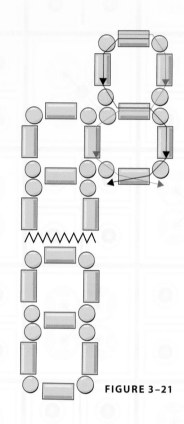

FIGURE 3–21

starting the second row

1 On the thread closest to the end of the weaving, pick up 1 seed and 1 bugle (Figure 3–19).

2 On the 2nd needle, pick up 1 seed, 1 bugle, 1 seed, 1 bugle and 1 seed (Figure 3–19).

3 Pass the 2nd needle through the bugle you picked up on the 1st needle (Figure 3–19).

4 The threads should be coming out of the top of the square you just made.

5 On the left-hand needle (the one closest to the 1st row), thread on 1 seed, 1 bugle, 1 seed and 1 bugle (Figure 3–20).

6 On the right-hand needle, pick up 1 seed, 1 bugle and 1 seed (Figure 3–20).

7 Pass the right-hand needle through the last bugle you picked up on the 1st needle (Figure 3–20). Again, the thread should come out of the top of the piece. You have just increased this row by a square.

8 To finish the rest of the row, work the needles back around the last 2 squares you made (Figure 3–21). Be sure to follow around the squares, passing through all beads so the needles come out where shown.

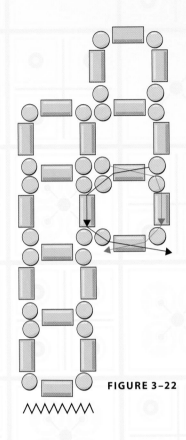

FIGURE 3–22

finishing the second row

1 On the left-hand needle (one closest to the 1st row), pick up 1 seed and pass through the bugle from the 1st row and pick up 1 seed.

2 On the other needle, pick up 1 seed, 1 bugle, 1 seed and 1 bugle.

3 Pass the 1st needle through the bugle you picked up on the 2nd needle (Figure 3–22).

4 Repeat Steps 1–3 down the row until you have 9 squares.

5 The threads will be coming out of the end of the row.

6 Work threads back around to the 2nd square up from the bottom and bring them out the side as shown in Figure 3–23.

7 Begin the 3rd row the same as you did in Figures 3–18 (page 39) and 3–19 (page 40).

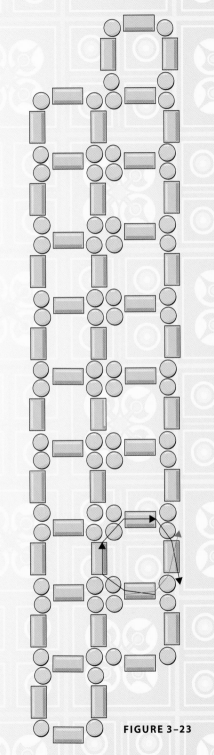

FIGURE 3–23

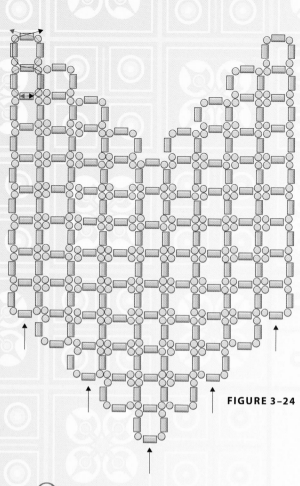

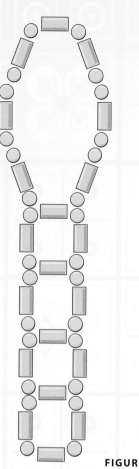

FIGURE 3–24

FIGURE 3–25

8
Work up the row, increasing by 1 square at the end (top) as you did in Figures 3–20 and 3–21 (page 40).

9
Continue until you have completed 5 rows.

10
Do 4 rows on the other side of the center row, being sure to make the chevron pattern shown in Figure 3–24.

adding the neck chain

1
Cut 4' (122cm) of thread and place a needle on each end.

2
Work the thread around the top 2 squares on 1 side as shown in Figure 3–24.

3
Weave enough squares to make a neck chain about 10" (25cm) long.

4
Make the last square by using the button as the end bugle bead. Pass around the end square several times to reinforce.
   Work thread tails into the beading, knot and trim excess thread.

5
Repeat Steps 1–5 on the other side of the pendant. When you get to the end, make a loop from bugles and seeds long enough to go around the button (Figure 3–25).

DETAIL OF BUTTON AND LOOP CLOSURE

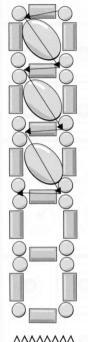

FIGURE 3-26

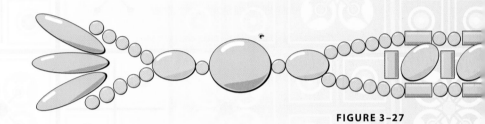

FIGURE 3-27

embellishing the piece

1 Single-thread 1 needle with 1 yard (1m) of thread.

2 Work the thread into the weaving at the end of the neck chain.

3 Refer to Figure 3–26. Bring the thread out of the end bugle. Pick up a 4mm fire polish bead and pass diagonally across the square. Pass through the next bugle from the opposite side.

4 Pick up a second 4mm fire polish bead and repeat.

5 Pass down the neck chain and the outside row of the pendant as shown in the project photo on page 38.

6 When done, work the thread around to the 3rd row over in the pendant and continue following Figure 3–26.

7 Embellish 1st, 3rd, 5th and 9th rows (shown by arrows in Figure 3–24, page 42) and the neck chain.

adding the dangles

1 On either side of the bugle, bring a new thread out of the 1st row bottom.

2 Following Figure 3–27, pick up 5 seeds, one 4mm, 1 seed, one 8mm, 1 seed, one 4mm, 5 seeds, 3 daggers and 5 seeds.

3 Pass the needle into the last 4mm bead you picked up and through the seed, 8mm, seed and 4mm beads.

4 Pick up 5 more seeds.

5 Pass back through the bottom bugle from the opposite side (Figure 3–27).

6 Move across the bottom of the piece doing a dangle on rows 1, 3, 5, 7 and 9.

7 Work thread tails into the beading. Knot and tie off threads. Trim excess thread.

Peyote Stitch

Peyote stitch has been around for centuries. It has several names, among them diagonal, twill and gourd stitch. Gourd stitch and peyote are the most common terms. *Peyote* is used by Native Americans to describe beadwork done with this stitch for religious and ceremonial purposes.

The beads in peyote stitch are offset like paving bricks. They are stacked on each other in vertical columns as the rows are made horizontally. Because the rows are offset by half of a bead, it is easier to count the rows on a diagonal.

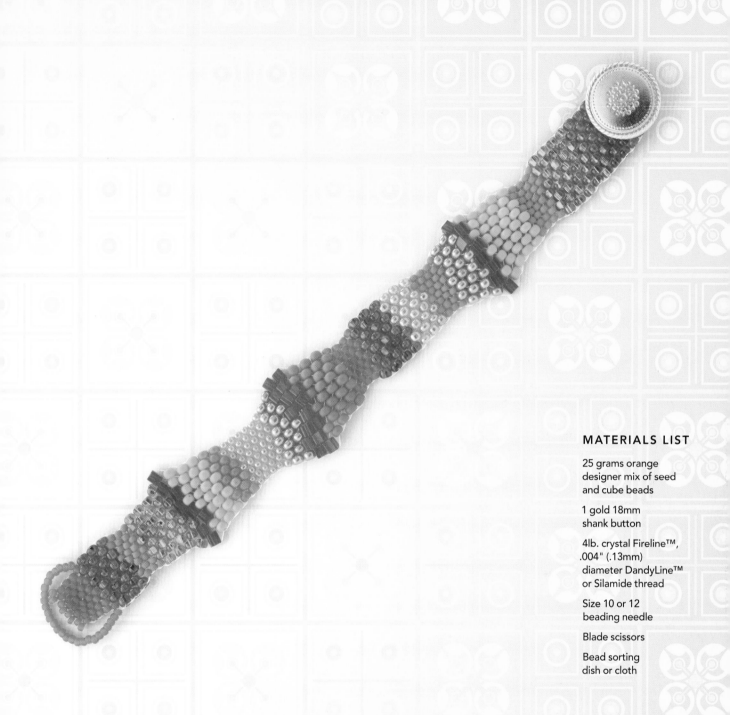

MATERIALS LIST

25 grams orange
designer mix of seed
and cube beads

1 gold 18mm
shank button

4lb. crystal Fireline™,
.004" (.13mm)
diameter DandyLine™
or Silamide thread

Size 10 or 12
beading needle

Blade scissors

Bead sorting
dish or cloth

orange designer mix bracelet

This bracelet is done with a designer mix of seed and 3mm cube beads using basic flat peyote weave. The different sizes of the beads create an undulating effect. If this bracelet was done in one bead size, it would become a straight band.

The instructions for the bracelet are for the basic flat peyote weave.

instructions

starting the weave

FIGURE 4–1

1 Separate the beads in the designer mix by size and color. Then choose 1 of the size 11° or 8° beads to start with.

2 Single-thread your needle with as much thread as you can handle and tie a stop bead within 6" (15cm) of the end of your thread.

3 Thread on 9 beads (Figure 4–1). These beads will count as the first 2 rows of your piece.

FIGURE 4–2

4 Refer to Figure 4–2, and pass your thread through the 3rd bead from the needle end. Hold the 3rd bead as you pass through it.

FIGURE 4–3

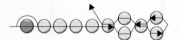

FIGURE 4–4

FIGURE 4–5

5 Pull the thread all the way through so that the 9th bead is resting on the 8th bead (Figure 4–3). You may have to move it into position.

6 Pick up another bead with your needle and pass through the 5th bead (Figure 4–4).

7 Continue in this manner until you get to the end of the row (Figure 4–5). Push each set of 2 beads together to tighten the work. You may remove the stop bead at this time and tie the 2 threads in a knot, or leave it and work the tail in later.

8 Your work should now have an up-and-down appearance. The beads that stick up are called "up-beads."

COUNTING ROWS

In doing a pattern in peyote stitch, keep in mind that the beads you string on at the very beginning become rows 1 and 2. When you go back along the row adding new beads, you are creating the third row. The third row beads push or pull the first two rows of beads into place.

As you progress in your pattern, keep close count of the rows—this is very important in following patterns. It may help to remember that each row is only a half-bead wide. Count your rows diagonally for a correct count.

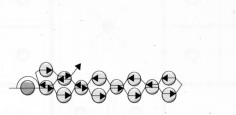

FIGURE 4–6

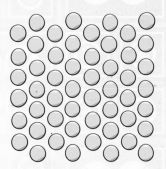

FIGURE 4–7

9 String on a new bead and pass through the 2nd bead from the end (an up-bead), as shown in Figure 4–6.

10 String on another bead and pass through the next up-bead. Continue to the end of the row, adding beads and rows in this manner until you have done about 7 rows. The pattern works up as shown in Figure 4–7.

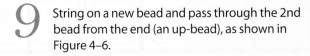

changing colors

1 When you have completed about 7–8 rows with the 1st color bead, change to a 2nd color. Refer to the photo on page 45.

2 This bracelet works best if you change the colors as well as the sizes of the beads, changing in the middle of the row or wherever you prefer. There is no right or wrong way to do this bracelet.
   Do not make all the sections the same length. Vary lengths as well as sizes of the beads.

3 Add new thread in the middle of the row using one of the knots on pages 12–14. Work the tails in. Knot, glue if desired and trim the excess thread.

4 Weave the bracelet to the desired length minus 2 rows, making sure to end with a section of the larger seeds.

adding the button

1 As you weave the next-to-last row, weave the shank of the button into the middle of the row in place of a bead. Weave 1 more row beyond the button shank.
   Work through the last couple of rows several times to reinforce the button.

2 Work thread tails in, knot, glue and trim the excess thread.

making the loop

1 Cut a new thread. Work it into the bracelet about ½" (13mm) from the end opposite the button. Bring the needle out 1 side of the band.

2 Pick up enough beads to make a loop long enough to go around the button with a little wiggle room. Remember that the loop will get tighter as you reinforce it.

3 Pass the loop to the other side of the bracelet. Work the needle through the beading and into the loop again. Pass through the loop several times to reinforce it.

4 Work thread tails in, knot, glue and trim excess thread.

MATERIALS LIST

1 round 26mm pendant
with bail (Christopher
Neal, see resources
list on page 140)

10 grams Cosmo Girl
Mix, size 11 beads
(Whimbeads.com)

90 burgundy metallic
seed beads, size 8

1 small silver
magnetic clasp

2 silver clamshell
bead tips

Two 2mm crimp beads

Brown Silamide thread

Size 10 or 12
beading needle

Bead sorting
dish or cloth

Scissors

ruffled pendant

Christopher Neal does amazing metal work. His pendants and clasps are beautifully crafted. This one appealed to me because it is both simple and intriguing. The colors are rich, and the designer bead mix matches extremely well.

The ruffle is accomplished by using a simple increase after completing a number of rows of regular peyote for a base. You can use the increase as you work to cover a three-dimensional object or if you just want to increase the size of your beading. Because I wanted a ruffle here, I used a lot of increases.

making the peyote band

1 Single-thread your needle with as much thread as you can handle.

2 Tie a waste bead within 6" (15cm) of the end of the thread.

3 Thread on 71 random beads from the Cosmo Girl Mix.

4 Refer to the basic flat peyote instructions in the *Orange Designer Mix Bracelet* project (pages 45–47) and weave a band 70 beads long and 7 rows wide.

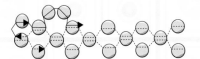

FIGURE 4–8

FIGURE 4–9

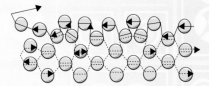

FIGURE 4–10

increasing the band

1 The simplest method of increasing peyote is to insert 2 beads in place of 1.

2 Turn the corner on the 8th row; after picking up a new bead to begin the row, pass through the 1st up-bead (Figure 4–8).

3 Next pick up 2 beads and pass through the next up-bead. Refer to Figure 4–8. Try to use 2 beads that are narrower than normal so they fit in better.

4 Pick up 1 bead and pass through the next bead (Figure 4–9).

5 For the 4th pass, pick up 2 beads. Refer to Figure 4–9.

6 Continue across the row doing a simple increase between every other up-bead until you've finished the 8th row. If you would like more ruffle, do 1 increase between every up-bead.

7 When you start the 9th row, work it as in basic flat peyote; add a bead between every up-bead (Figure 4–10), including between the 2 beads you picked up in each increase.

8 Weave an additional 4 rows, making a total of 12 rows.

9 Work the thread tail in. Knot and glue the thread end and trim the excess thread.

making the necklace

1 Cut 1 yard (1m) of thread and double-thread your needle.

2 Tie a crimp securely to the end of the thread.

3 Glue the knot and trim the tail.

4 Insert the needle through the clamshell from the inside out. Close the clamshell around the crimp and knot.

5 Begin threading on 1 seed from the Cosmo Girl Mix (the sample uses a burgundy metallic seed), alternating with 1 size 8 bead until you have 45 of the larger beads strung. End with a small seed.

6 Pass the needle through the end up-bead on the straight edge of the peyote ruffle.

7 Pick up a small seed and pass through the next up-bead in the band.

8 Continue across the band in this manner until you get to the opposite side.

9 Repeat Steps 4 and 5 in reverse order.

10 Pass through the clamshell from the outside in.

11 Cut the thread from the needle; thread a crimp on 1 piece of the thread.

12 Tie off the threads against the crimp. Glue, knot and trim the thread ends.

13 Close the clamshell around the knot.

14 Bend the bar of 1 clamshell around the loop on the clasp. Repeat for the other end.

15 Place the pendant on the center of the ruffle. You may have to roll the beading to get it to go through the pendant bail.

MATERIALS LIST

One ¾" × 2⅝"
(2cm × 7cm) foam
fishing bobber

10 grams purple AB
size 11° seed beads

20 grams gold-plated
size 11° seed beads

20 grams purple matte
size 11° seed beads

10 grams purple
aurora borealis (AB)
size 8° seed beads

1 round gold
10mm bead

1 spool Beadalon®
DandyLine™ .004"
(.13mm) diameter black
thread or 4lb. Fireline™

Size 10 or 12
beading needle

Bead sorting
dish or cloth

Blade scissors

Gem adhesive (I
use Gem-Tac™)

Chain nose pliers

Permanent Adhesive
(by Beacon Adhesives)

Acrylic paint (black
or color to match
your beads)

Paintbrush

fishing bobber necklace

The "bobber" in this necklace is a large foam fishing bobber. It was originally florescent orange, but a quick coat of paint turned it black—a much better color to bead over.

Since bobbers come in a great many sizes, shapes and colors, you may not be able to find the exact one used in the project, so be prepared to alter the pattern to fit your bobber. You will need to practice peyote stitch, especially decreasing it, as you will have to figure out the decreases for your particular bobber as you weave. The neck strap is a spiral rope, but you can use any necklace of your choice.

instructions

FIGURE 4–11

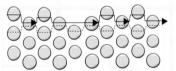

FIGURE 4–12

beading the bobber

1 If your bobber has a stick in the middle, remove it carefully.

2 Paint the bobber black or a color to match your beads. Let it dry completely.

3 Single-thread your needle with as much thread as you think you can handle.

4 Refer to the beading diagram, Figure 4–11, and the basic flat peyote diagrams on pages 46–47.

5 Thread on 40 purple size 11° seeds.

6 Tie the beads in a loop around the middle of the bobber. Check for size. The beads should fit snugly around the middle of the bobber. If you need to adjust the number of beads, do so now. Adjust the pattern accordingly.

7 The 40 beads you threaded on are the middle 2 rows of the pattern. Step up through the 1st bead you picked up to start the 3rd row on 1 side.

8 Following the pattern, begin weaving on 1 side of the center 2 rows of beads until the bobber decreases in size so that your beading no longer fits snugly.

9 Decrease as needed to keep the beading snug against the bobber. To decrease, refer to Figure 4–12.

Where you need the decrease, do not add a bead; pass your thread through 2 up-beads, and pull the beads up tightly together. Note you are working in a ring, but the illustrations are shown flat. You will be passing around the ring in the same direction.

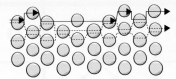

FIGURE 4–13

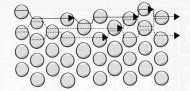

FIGURE 4–14

10 On the next row around the bobber, add just 1 bead in place of the 2 (Figure 4–13).

11 As you continue, work the next row as usual (Figure 4–14). You have decreased the row by 2 beads. Do this where you feel it necessary to maintain the snug fit of the beading.

12 Complete both sides of the pattern and tie off the threads. Glue the knots, and trim the thread ends.

embellishing the bobber

1 Add a new thread. Come out in the center row between 2 beads. Pick up a gold size 11° seed. Pass into the next bead in the center row. Continue around the bobber, picking up a gold seed in between each bead in the center row. Refer to the photo on page 51.

2 Repeat Step 1 on either side of the center band of purple AB and gold seeds using a gold bead. Refer to the photo on page 51 for placement.

3 Repeat Step 1 with purple matte size 11° seeds in the section between the gold stripes. Refer to the photo on page 51 for placement. Set the bobber aside.

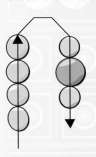

FIGURE 4–15

weaving the spiral rope necklace

1 Single-thread your needle with as much thread as you think you can handle.

2 For the rope, use the purple matte as the core bead and 2 gold seeds and 1 purple AB size 8° seed as the outside beads.

It is not necessary to use a stop bead, as you will go back through the beginning beads in your 1st pass-through.

3 Pick up 4 purple matte (core beads), 1 gold seed, 1 purple AB size 8° seed and 1 gold seed (outside beads) (Figure 4–15).

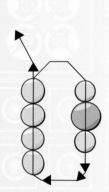

FIGURE 4–16

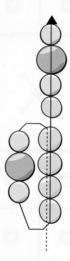

FIGURE 4–17

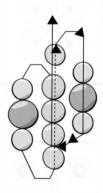

FIGURE 4–18

4 Pass back through the 4 core beads (Figure 4–16). Pull snug. Push the outside beads to the left.

5 Thread on 1 purple matte (core bead), 1 gold seed, 1 purple AB size 8° seed and 1 gold seed (Figure 4–17).

6 Skip the 1st core bead and pass the needle through the next 3 core beads from the bottom up (Figure 4–18).

7 Pass through the core bead you picked up in Step 6. Pull snug. Push the outside beads to the left.

8 Add 1 core bead and the gold/8/gold combination.

making the clasp

When you are done weaving the rope, make a bead and loop closure.

1 On 1 end of the rope, thread on the large (10 mm) gold bead and a purple matte seed.

2 Skip the seed and pass back through the large gold bead.

3 Work the thread into the rope and back through the beads several times to reinforce.

4 Work the thread into the rope. Tie off and glue the knots. Trim the thread ends.

5 On other end, thread on 2 purple matte seeds, then enough to go around the large gold bead.

6 Pass the needle back through the first 2 beads you picked up. Check the loop for size to make sure it goes over the large gold bead.

7 Work the thread though the rope and back through the loop several times to reinforce.

8 Work the thread into the rope. Tie off and glue the knots. Trim the thread ends.

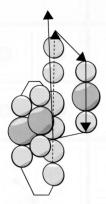

FIGURE 4–19

9 Skip the bottom 2 core beads and pass back through the 3 core beads above that and the 1 you just added. Pull up snug. Push the outside beads to the left (Figure 4–19).

10 Continue in this manner until you have half the length you need.

11 Thread on enough beads to equal the length of the bobber. Pass through the bobber.

12 Continue weaving the spiral rope on the other side of the bobber, keeping the thread that passes through the bobber tight as you begin the new section of weaving.

Square Stitch

Square stitch is a very good basic stitch to know. It looks just like loom weaving when it's finished, but you don't have all those warp threads to work into the piece. Square stitch is also more portable. Dragging a loom around can be cumbersome, but with square stitch, you can add a fringe, increase and decrease and generally do all of the things you can do on the loom.

The downside of square stitch is that it is much slower to do than loom work because you add one bead at a time. It is possible to add more than one bead, but it doesn't have as nice a finished look as the single-bead method.

The projects in this section will teach you how to use different sizes of beads and how to increase and decrease the stitch to weave shaped pieces. First, I've provided a refresher course on how to do basic square stitch.

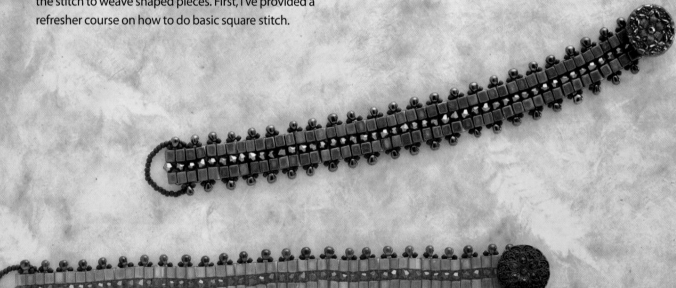

demonstration: square stitch

Square stitch looks just like loom weaving, without all those warp threads to work in. You can add a fringe, increase and decrease, and generally do all the things you can do on the loom.

The following is a refresher on how to do basic square stitch.

FIGURE 5–1

1 Single-thread your needle and tie a stop bead within a few inches of the end.

2 Refer to Figure 5–1. Pick up 5 beads on your needle. Take them to the end of your thread.

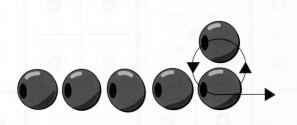

FIGURE 5–2

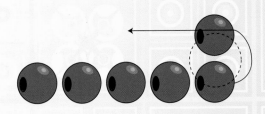

FIGURE 5–3

3 Pick up 1 bead. Refer to Figure Figure 5–2. Pass thread back through the last bead of the 5 you just picked up.

4 Then pass the thread through the 6th bead again. Pull up snug until the 6th bead sits on the 5th bead (Figure 5–3).

FIGURE 5–4

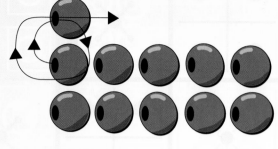

FIGURE 5–5

5 Pick up the 7th bead. Pass the thread into the 4th bead and back up and through the 7th bead. Continue across the row in this manner (Figure 5–4).

6 When you have completed a row, go down and through the previous row, and then back up through the just-finished row to reinforce it and keep your work lined up. This helps keep everything straight if you are using Delicas or Japanese seeds in which the holes are quite large.

7 Turn the next corner by picking up the 11th bead. Pass thread through the 10th bead and back through the eleventh bead (Figure 5–5).

8 Continue weaving back and forth across the row in this manner until you have the size you want.

ABSTRACT NECKLACE

This abstract necklace first appeared on the cover of Jewelry Crafts Magazine. *The woven pendant is done in square stitch with seed beads.*

crystals, cubes & drops bracelet

This bracelet uses three popular types of beads: crystals, cubes and tiny teardrops. The weave is a combination of square stitch and stringing. These bracelets work up quickly, so you can make them in several colors for yourself or as gifts. You may find that using both matte and shiny beads gives the pattern depth and character.

Length: 7" (18cm)

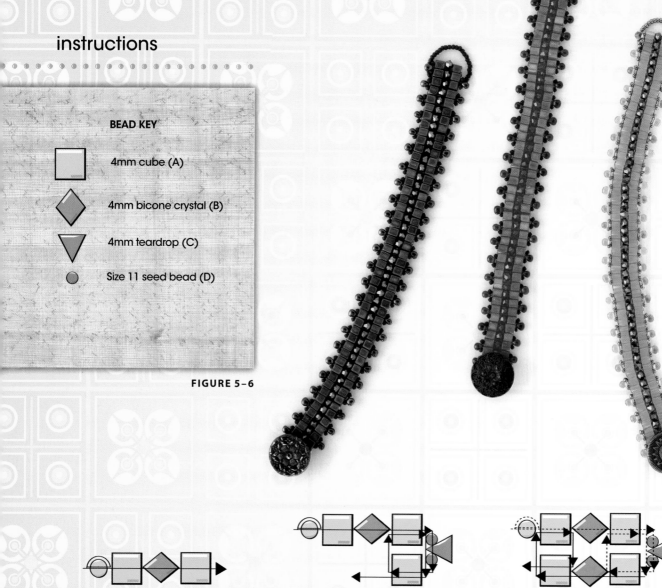

BEAD KEY

☐ 4mm cube (A)

◇ 4mm bicone crystal (B)

▽ 4mm teardrop (C)

● Size 11 seed bead (D)

FIGURE 5-6

FIGURE 5-7

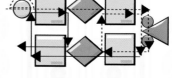

FIGURE 5-8

FIGURE 5-9

weaving the basic band

1 Single-thread your needle with 2 yards (2m) of thread.

2 Tie a stop bead on the end leaving an 8" (20cm) tail.

3 Pick up 1 cube bead (A), 1 crystal (B) and 1 cube bead (A). Refer to the Bead Key (Figure 5-6) and to Figure 5-7.

4 Next, pick up 1 seed (D), 1 teardrop (C), 1 seed (D) and 1 cube (A).

5 Refer to Figure 5-8 and pass the thread back through the 2nd (A) bead you picked up, across under the (D)/(C)/(D) beads and back into the 3rd (A) you picked up. Pull snug.

6 Pick up 1 (B) and 1 (A) bead.

7 Refer to Figure 5-9 and pass into the 1st (A) bead you picked up, then across and back through the last (A) you picked up. Pull snug but not tight. You need to allow a little wiggle room so the cubes will move against each other.

8 Pick up 1 (D) bead, 1 (C), 1 (D) and 1 (A).

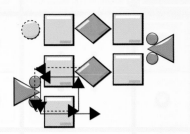

FIGURE 5–10

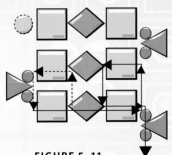

FIGURE 5–11

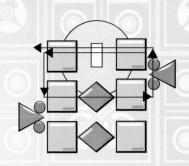

FIGURE 5–12

adding the button

9 Refer to Figure 5–10. Pass across to the 4th (A) bead you picked up and pass through and back into the 5th (A) and pull snug.

10 Pick up 1 (B) bead and 1 (A) and pass across and through the 4th (A) you picked up and back into the 6th (A) (Figure 5–11).

11 Pick up 1 (D) bead, 1 (C), 1 (D) and 1 (A). Pass across and through the 6th (A) and back under the (D)/(C)/(D) combination and through the 7th (A) (Figure 5–11).

12 Continue following Steps 3–11 until you are 1 row short of the length you need.

1 In the last row you weave, the shank of the button replaces the crystal (B). Pick it up just like you would the (B) (Figure 5–12).

2 Work the thread around the end couple of rows until you have passed through the button several times. Tie off the thread. Glue the knots and trim the excess thread.

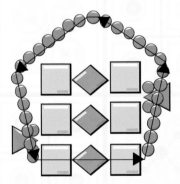

FIGURE 5–13

adding the loop

1 Work a new thread into the other end of the bracelet down a few rows from the end.

2 Come out on the side of the 3rd row back from the end. Pick up enough (D) beads to make a loop big enough to pass over the button without being too loose (Figure 5–13).

3 Pass back through the 3rd row, across and through the loop again. Repeat once more, if possible, to reinforce the loop.

4 Work thread into the piece. Knot, glue and trim the thread ends.

MATERIALS LIST

4 grams brown aurora borealis (AB) size 11 seed beads

1 gram green size 14 silver-lined seed beads

15 opaque yellow size 14 seed beads

15 assorted color 5.5mm crystal Margarites

1 purple aurora borealis (AB) 7mm × 9mm butterfly bead

Two 2" (5cm) squares black synthetic suede

One 1¾" (4cm) square of plastic (margarine carton lid)

One 1¼" (3cm) pin back

4lb. Fireline™ or .004" (.13mm) diameter DandyLine™

Fabric glue (I use Fabri-Tac™ Fabric Glue)

Blade scissors

Bead sorting dish or cloth

flower basket brooch

The basket in this embroidered brooch is done in square stitch. Because the weaving starts with the bottom row, the basket teaches you how to increase square stitch at the ends of the rows. The flowers are crystal Margarites held on with seed bead centers, and the leaves and stems are embroidered seed beads. The edging is a picot stitch, which you will find useful in finishing several of the projects in the book.

Size: 2" (5cm) square

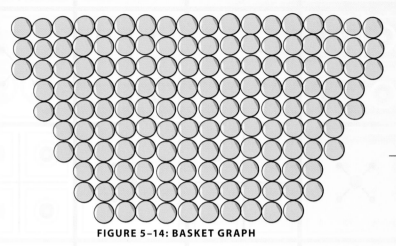

FIGURE 5–14: BASKET GRAPH

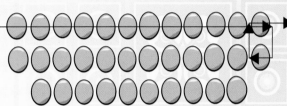

FIGURE 5–16

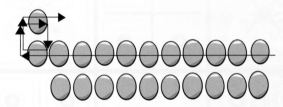

FIGURE 5–15

weaving the basket

1 Single-thread your needle with about 1½ yards (1m) of thread.

2 Tie on a stop bead, leaving an 8" (20cm) tail.

3 Refer to Figure 5–14 for the basket graph.

4 Pick up 10 of the brown seeds and take them to the end of your thread against the stop bead.

5 Refer to the *Square Stitch* demonstration on pages 57–58 and weave the next row as shown.

6 Pass through the bottom row and up through the row you just finished to reinforce.

7 To start the 3rd row and to increase the 2nd row by 1 bead, pick up 2 beads.

8 Refer to Figure 5–15. Pass the thread back through the 1st bead as shown and into the 2nd bead again, so that the 2nd bead you added sits on the 1st bead—you have lengthened the row by 1 bead width.

9 Continue adding beads as you have all along to make the 3rd row.

10 When you get to the other end, you need to extend the 3rd row by 1 bead as well as the 2nd row. To do that, pick up 2 beads.

11 Refer to Figure 5–16. Pass the needle back up through the 1st new bead you picked up (making a loop) which is the end of the 3rd row.

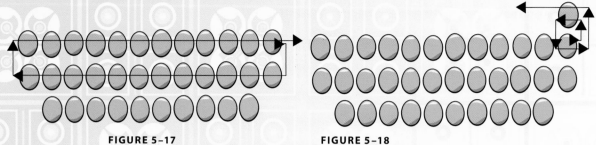

FIGURE 5-17　　　　**FIGURE 5-18**

12 Pass back into the 2nd new bead and down through the 2nd row to reinforce. Then pass the thread through the length of the 3rd row as shown in Figure 5–17.

13 Begin the 4th row by adding a new bead as shown in Figure 5–18. Continue to work back and forth across the piece, adding extra beads at the end of the rows as explained in the preceding steps.

14 Work your thread into the piece. Tie half hitch knots to secure, glue the thread end if desired and trim the excess thread.

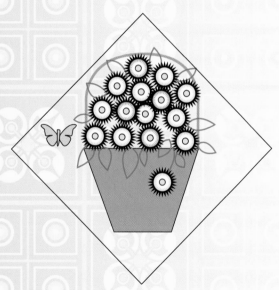

FIGURE 5-19

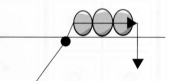

FIGURE 5-20

attaching the basket

1 Single-thread your needle and tack the completed basket diagonally on 1 piece of suede as shown in Figure 5–19. Be sure to tack it securely at all 4 corners and in the middle.

2 To backstitch the handle in place, bring the thread to the front at 1 corner of the basket. Pick up 3 brown seeds and lay them in a straight line up from the basket. Pass the needle back into the suede at the end of the beads (Figure 5–20).

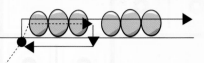

FIGURE 5–21

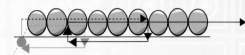

FIGURE 5–22

3 Come back through in the 1st hole and pass through the beads again and pick up 3 new beads (Figure 5–21).

4 Pass back into the suede at the end of the beads.

5 Bring your needle up through the 4th bead from the end (the 3rd bead of the first 3) and go up through the suede, through this bead and the last 3 you picked up. Pick up 3 more (Figure 5–22).

6 Continue picking up 3 beads and passing back through 4 as you make the handle. Refer to Figure 5–19 (page 64) and make the handle curve as you add beads.

7 Secure in the back of the work.

adding the flowers, leaves and butterfly

1 Bring the thread up from the back and pass through a Margarite and a yellow size 14 seed. Skip the seed and pass back through the Margarite. Pass to the next flower and repeat; refer to Figure 5–19 on page 64 for placement. Be sure to add the flower on the lower basket.

2 Use a single-thread and size 14 green seeds to make stems and leaves. Refer to Figure 5–19 on page 64 for placement. Come up from the under-side and thread on enough beads to make the stem or leaf. Pass back into the work. Tack the stems and leaves into place by coming up from behind and over the thread between the beads and back into the work to hold the thread where you want it.

3 Sew the butterfly bead to the side of the basket. Pass through it several times and tie off on the back.

finishing the brooch

1 Glue the piece of plastic centered on the back of the embroidered piece.

2 The pin should go in the upper back of the remaining piece of suede. Measure to see where the ends of the pin go. Make a narrow slit at each end so the pin ends will pass through with the bar under the backing.

3 Glue the backing to the remainder of the pin.

4 Carefully trim the edges to straighten.

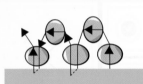

FIGURE 5–23

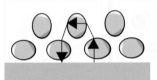

FIGURE 5–24

making the picot edging

1 To make the picot edge, cut about 1 yard (1m) of thread. Single-thread your needle and knot the end. Trim close to the knot.

2 Work the knot in between the layers of suede close to an edge in the middle of 1 side of the brooch.

3 Pick up 3 brown seeds.

4 Come up from the back side of the brooch about 1/16" (2mm) from the edge and through to the front of the piece about 2 beads' space away from where you started.

5 Pass through the 3rd seed from the bottom up (Figure 5–23). Pull snug.

6 Pick up 2 brown seeds and repeat Steps 4–5. See Figure 5–21 on page 65.

7 Repeat around the outside edge of the piece.

8 When you get back to where you started, pick up 1 brown seed and pass into the very 1st seed you picked up (Figure 5–24).

9 Work in the thread tails, knot, glue and trim.

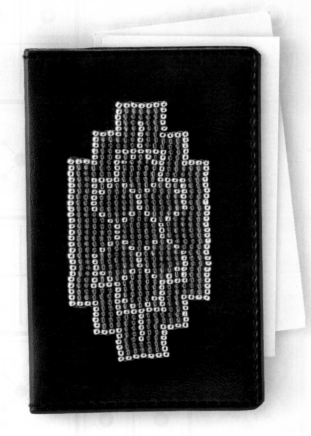

MATERIALS LIST

1 business card case

5 grams gold-plated size 11° Japanese seed beads

3 grams fuchsia silver-lined size 11° Japanese seed beads

3 grams teal silver-lined size 11° Japanese seed beads

1 gram green silver-lined size 11° Japanese seed beads

4lb. Fireline™ or .004" (.13mm) diameter DandyLine™ (black)

Adhesive (I use Gem-Tac™ Permanent Adhesive)

Blade scissors

Bead sorting dish or cloth

Fine grit sandpaper

1 sheet copy paper

Heavy books

square-stitched card case

A lot of things can be improved by adding beads. Such is the case with this plain black business card case. Wouldn't this beaded one be a lot nicer to pull out of your purse than a plain one? Look around for cross-stitch patterns that work well for square stitch—you could personalize this idea any way you want.

The object of this project is to learn how to decrease square stitch. You can do both increasing and decreasing on this one, but if you start in the middle and work to the top and bottom, all you have to remember how to do is decrease. Decreasing is a lot easier than increasing.

instructions

BEAD KEY

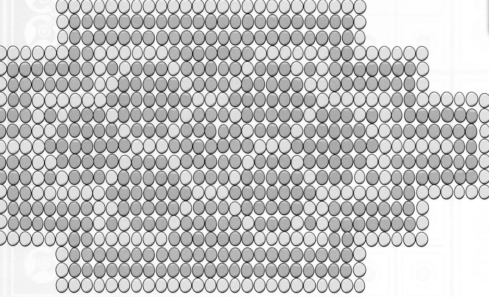

FIGURE 5–25A

⊙⊙	Gold
⊙⊙	Fuchsia
⊙⊙	Teal
⊙⊙	Green

FIGURE 5–25B

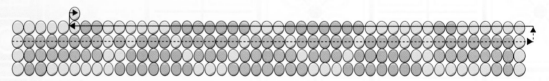

FIGURE 5–26

weaving the medallion

1   Cut as much thread as you can handle and single-thread your needle.

2   Tie a stop bead on the end, leaving an 8" (20cm) tail.

3   Start by threading on the beads for the long center row referring to the bead placement graph (Figure 5–25A, above).

4   Refer to *Demonstration: Square Stitch*, pages 57–58, and begin weaving the pattern. Be careful that you follow the pattern closely as there are a lot of color changes.

5   Work the center long row and the next 3, which will be the same length—45 beads. Also, remember to pass back through the rows to reinforce.

6   When you get to the 5th row, you need to decrease.

As you are passing back through the 4th row to reinforce, stop 5 beads back from the end as shown in Figure 5–26 and bring your needle up from between the 5th and 6th beads from the end of the row. Pick up a gold-plated seed as shown.

FIGURE 5–27

7 Pass back into the 4th row through the gold bead (6th one in from the end) and back up and through the gold-plated see you just added (Figure 5–27).

8 Continue weaving the pattern as before, decreasing where you need to.

9 When you are done with the 1st half of the weaving, do the 2nd half in the same manner.

10 Work the thread tails in. Knot and glue the thread end, and trim the excess thread.

attaching the medallion

1 Carefully sand the area where the medallion will be on the front of the card case to rough up the surface.

2 Very carefully spread a fine layer of glue on one side of the medallion.

3 Position the medallion on the card case.

4 Lay the card case on a hard surface with the beaded side up.

5 Place paper over the beading and put heavy books on top.

6 Allow to lie undisturbed overnight until glue is dry.

DETAIL OF MEDALLION
This is the section of the medallion illustrated by Figures 5–26 (page 68) and 5–27 (this page).

Vertical Netting

Vertical netting is an excellent weave to cover objects, especially round objects, because it expands and contracts nicely to fit a shape. Vertical netting resembles a net with diamond-shaped holes. The weave is constructed by weaving up and down the piece vertically. (Weaving can also be done horizontally, but that will not be covered here.)

The diamond-shaped holes vary in size according to how many beads are used in each section. The beads in the sections are sometimes called bridge beads, while the beads that connect the diamonds are called shared beads. Always use an odd number of sections, because the diamonds fit together in an offset pattern. The pattern will not work with an even number of sections.

MATERIALS LIST

2 black 20mm round plastic beads

6 grams white size 11° pearl seed beads

3 grams gold-plated size 11° seed beads

4 black 6mm bicone crystals

Two 2" (5cm) gold head pins

7 links 4mm round link gold chain

1 pair gold ear wires

Size 10 or 12 beading needle

2 yards (2m) Crystal 4lb. Fireline™ or .004" (.13mm) diameter DandyLine™ white

Adhesive (I use Gem-Tac™ Permananet Adhesive)

Round nose pliers

Wire cutters

Scissors

beaded bead earrings

Vertical netting covers two 20mm round plastic beads to make this pair of earrings. I used plastic beads because they are lightweight—which is important if you are hanging them from your ears!

Follow the basic project instructions to make these earrings: A simple net is woven, joined into a tube, gathered at the top, placed on the bead and gathered at the bottom. However, if you want to cover something other than a 20mm bead, experiment to see how many patterns you will need and how many beads to put in each pattern. The project instructions serve as a guideline. Netting can have a million variables, all of which will work. Be sure the first row of the net is slightly longer than the object you want to cover as the net will shrink up some when you place it over the object.

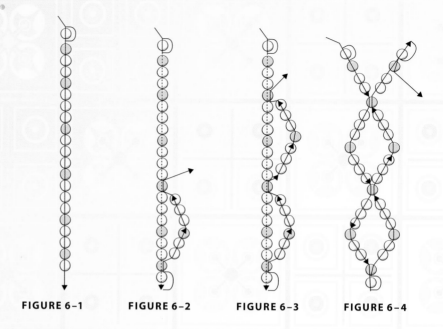

FIGURE 6–1   FIGURE 6–2   FIGURE 6–3   FIGURE 6–4

making the net

1 Cut 1 yard (1m) of thread and single thread your needle.

2 Using a half hitch knot that you can remove later, tie on a white seed, leaving an 8" (20cm) tail.

3 Refer to Figure 6–1 and pick up 1 gold seed (the shared bead), 2 white (the bridge beads), 1 gold, 3 white, 1 gold, 3 white, 1 gold, 3 white, 1 gold, 2 white, 1 gold and 1 white to make Row 1.

4 Skip the last white bead and pass back through the last (shared) gold bead from the bottom up (Figure 6–2).

5 Pick up 2 white, 1 gold and 3 white beads and pass through the 3rd gold bead up from the bottom from the underside up (Figure 6–2).

6 Pick up 3 white, 1 gold nd 3 white beads and pass through the 5th gold bead from the bottom from the underside up as shown in Figure 6–3.

7 Pick up 2 white, 1 gold and 1 white bead as shown in Figure 6–4 to finish Row 2.

TIP

You will be creating points at the tops and bottoms of the piece. This is how you count the number of rows you need to cover an object. For example, if you need nine rows to go around an item like the bead used in these earrings, you would work the piece until you had nine points top and bottom. Keep in mind that the beginning half-point and the ending half-point are included in that number. When you join the net into a tube, those points will work into the piece.

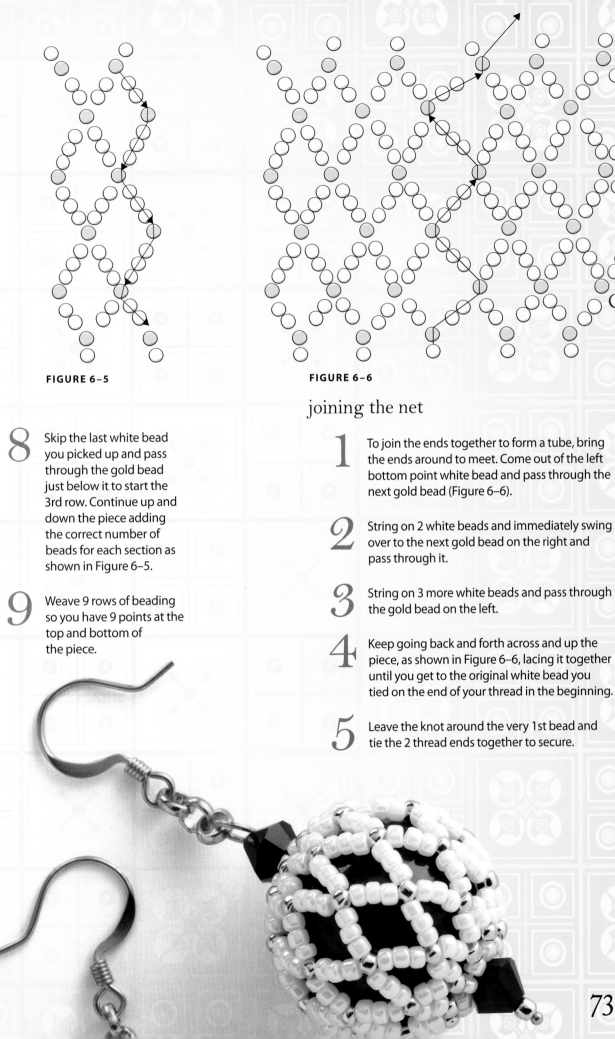

FIGURE 6–5

FIGURE 6–6

joining the net

8 Skip the last white bead you picked up and pass through the gold bead just below it to start the 3rd row. Continue up and down the piece adding the correct number of beads for each section as shown in Figure 6–5.

9 Weave 9 rows of beading so you have 9 points at the top and bottom of the piece.

1 To join the ends together to form a tube, bring the ends around to meet. Come out of the left bottom point white bead and pass through the next gold bead (Figure 6–6).

2 String on 2 white beads and immediately swing over to the next gold bead on the right and pass through it.

3 String on 3 more white beads and pass through the gold bead on the left.

4 Keep going back and forth across and up the piece, as shown in Figure 6–6, lacing it together until you get to the original white bead you tied on the end of your thread in the beginning.

5 Leave the knot around the very 1st bead and tie the 2 thread ends together to secure.

covering the 20mm bead

1. Using your working thread if you have enough (add a new one on if you don't), pass through all the white point beads and gather into a ring.

2. Pass through all point beads again. Tie a few half hitch knots and work the thread to the other end of the netting, following the pattern.

3. Place on the 20mm bead so the ring of point beads matches up with the hole in the big bead.

4. Run the needle through all the point beads on that end and pull up tight. Pass through again.

5. Tie half hitch knots and work the tail of the thread into the work. Glue the knot and trim the excess thread.

6. Repeat all steps for the 2nd earring.

making the earrings

1. On 1 head pin, thread on 1 gold seed, 1 black crystal, 1 beaded bead and 1 black crystal.

2. Trim the pin to 3/8" (10mm) and turn a loop on the top.

3. Cut the 7-link piece of chain in half so you have two 3-link pieces.

4. Attach a head pin to 1 end link of a chain piece.

5. Attach the other end of the chain to the ear wire.

6. Repeat for the other earring.

THE VERSATILITY OF BEADED BEADS

You can make a pendant exactly like the *Beaded Bead Earrings*, stringing the bead on a head pin pendant bail and hanging the pendant on a chain.

There are any number of combinations of colors and ways to use beaded beads. You can also embellish on top of the netting to make it richer looking.

MATERIALS LIST

15 grams silver-lined gold size 11° seed beads

32 orange double aurora borealis (AB) 6mm bicone crystals

63 bronze 4mm bicone crystals

5 grams bronze metallic size 11° seed beads

1 small gold triangle toggle clasp

2 gold clamshell bead tips

4 gold 4mm jump rings

1 size 10 or 12 beading needle

4lb. crystal Fireline™ or .004" (.13mm) diameter white DandyLine™

Blade scissors

Bead sorting dish or cloth

Jewelry pliers

gold netted necklace

One of the best things about the beading community is all the marvelously talented people you get to meet. Most are very generous in sharing their experience and knowledge. One of my favorites is Diane Fitzgerald. When I asked her if I could share her secrets for increasing and decreasing netting as shown in her book, *Netted Beadwork* (Interweave Press, Inc., 2003), she very graciously agreed. If you find you like this weave, I suggest you get a copy of Diane's book as it is an excellent resource on netting.

This necklace is meant to fold over on itself. You can adjust the length and width of the netting.

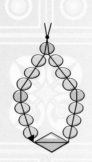

FIGURE 6–7

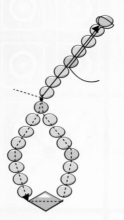

FIGURE 6–8

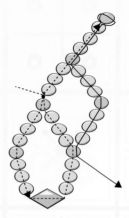

FIGURE 6–9

beginning the net

1 Single-thread the needle with as much thread as you can handle.

2 Pick up 1 bronze seed (shared bead), 3 silver-lined gold seeds (bridge beads), 1 bronze seed, 3 silver-lined gold seeds, 1 bronze crystal, 3 silver-lined gold seeds, 1 bronze seed and 3 silver-lined gold seeds. Take them to the end of the thread and tie the threads together in a double knot, leaving an 8" (20cm) tail (Figure 6–7).

3 Thread on 3 silver-lined gold seeds and 1 bronze seed twice as shown in Figure 6–8, making a spike. Skip the last bronze seed and pass through the next 3 silver-lined gold seeds and 1 bronze seed as shown.

4 Pick up 3 silver-lined gold seeds, 1 bronze seed and 3 silver-lined gold seeds and pass through the bronze seed as shown in Figure 6–9.

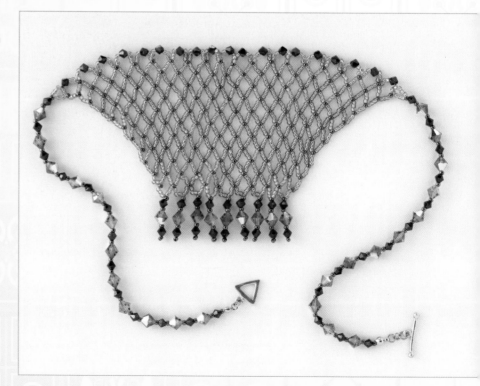

GOLD NETTED NECKLACE, UNROLLED
This shows the actual shape of the finished necklace.

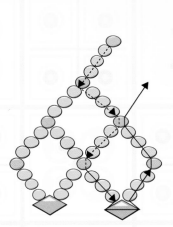

FIGURE 6–10

FIGURE 6–11

FIGURE 6–12

5 Pick up 3 silver-lined gold seeds, 1 bronze 4mm bicone crystal, 3 silver-lined gold seeds, 1 bronze seed and 3 silver-lined gold seeds and pass through the bronze seed as shown in Figure 6–10.

6 Pick up 3 silver-lined gold seeds, 1 bronze seed and 3 silver-lined gold seeds and pass through the bronze seed on the point as shown in Figure 6–11.

7 Continue adding spikes as in Figure 6-8 on page 76, working up and down the piece until you have made 10 diamonds (patterns) on the beginning side.

8 To make the 1st fringe, pick up 3 silver-lined gold seeds, 1 bronze seed, 1 bronze 4mm bicone crystal, 1 bronze seed, 1 orange AB 6mm double bicone crystal, 1 bronze seed, 1 bronze 4mm bicone crystal and 1 bronze seed. Skip the last bronze seed and pass back through all the beads you picked up, except the 3 silver-lined gold seeds you picked up first (Figure 6–12).

FIGURE 6–13

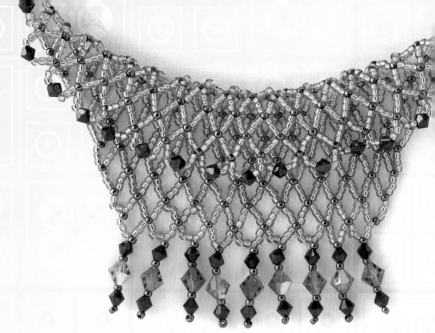

9 Pick up 3 silver-lined gold seeds, 1 bronze seed and 3 silver-lined gold seeds and work back down the triangle as before (Figure 6–13).

10 Work back up to the fringe end, add a short spike and make another fringe as you did in Step 8. Repeat Steps 8 and 9 until you have made 9 fringe strands.

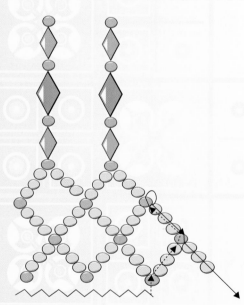

FIGURE 6–14

ending the net

1 The next time you come back down the side of the net, instead of making a fringe, loop the thread around the bronze seed (Figure 6–14) and pass back through the 3 silver-lined gold seeds and the next bronze seed on the side of the net as shown.

2 Continue working up and down the side of the net, making each pass 1 diamond shorter until you end with the diamond with the bronze 4mm bicone crystal—this is the end diamond.

3 Work the thread into the piece. Tie a few half hitch knots, glue the thread end and trim the excess thread.

making the necklace

1 Cut 20" (51cm) of thread and single-thread the needle.

2 Pass the needle through the silver-lined gold seeds between the bronze 4mm bicone crystal and the bronze seed on the upper corner of the net. Refer to the photo on pages 75 and 76 for placement.

3 Place the 2nd end of the thread through the needle so your needle is now double-threaded.

4 Alternately pick up 1 bronze seed, 1 bronze 4mm bicone crystal , 1 bronze seed and 1 orange AB 6mm double bicone crystal until you have 12 orange crystals threaded.

5 End with 1 bronze seed, 1 bronze 4mm bicone crystal and 1 bronze seed.

6 Pass the needle through a clamshell bead tip from the underside.

7 Remove 1 thread from the needle.

8 Pick up a crimp.

9 Tie the threads off against the crimp, making sure the beads are snug and no thread shows.

10 Glue the knot. Trim the thread ends and close the clamshell around the knot. Bend the bar of the clamshell into a loop.

11 Attach the loop end of the toggle to the clamshell with a jump ring.

12 Repeat Steps 1–10 for the other side of the necklace.

13 Hook 1 jump ring to the clamshell bead tip and 1 to the bar end of the toggle.

14 Use the last jump ring to attach the clamshell to the bar end of the toggle.

BRONZE/GREEN NETTED NECKLACE
Another beautiful example of vertical netting.

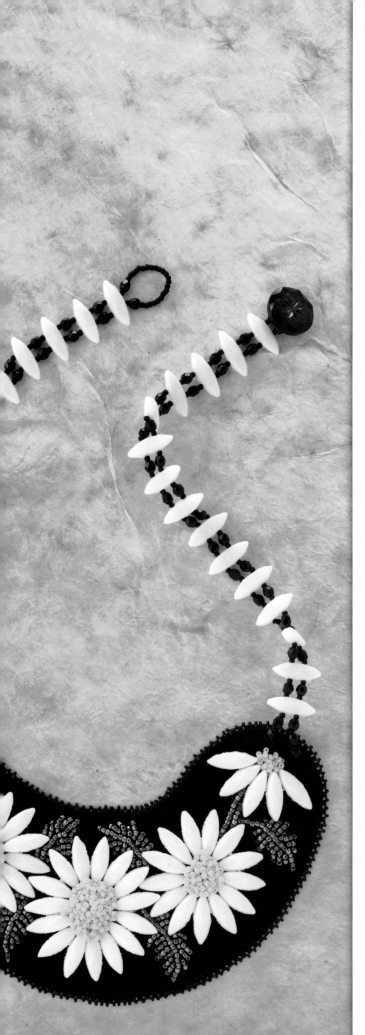

working with the unusual

I have one of those minds that constantly thinks "outside the box." Putting things together that normally would never go together or using common things in uncommon ways fuels my creativity. I love incorporating non-jewelry items in my beading or making jewelry with items normally used for other pursuits. In fact, my first book for Krause Publications (*Beaded Jewelry with Found Objects*, 2004) was based on that premise. In it, I used all sorts of unusual items like gourds, drawer knobs, even rubber fishing worms to make elegant beaded jewelry. It sounds strange, but it works. Exciting possibilities exist everywhere if you are only open to looking for them.

The projects that follow in this section require a certain amount of thinking "outside the box" on your part. You may not to be able to find all the materials to make the projects exactly as shown here, but you can find similar items. The patterns provided were designed to get you to thinking about different ways to use things that you have on hand or that you find as you progress on your beading journey. Unusual handmade items, hardware store discoveries, fishing tackle or even jewelry findings can be used to make stunning jewelry. All it takes is the willingness to look beyond the norm and the urge to experiment combined with the information given in this section.

Have a great time exploring the possibilities!

Embroider Those Beads

It is my contention that there is very little (within reason, of course) that can't be improved by adding beads. Such is certainly the case with clothing. Beads add sparkle and depth to fabric and leather. You can stitch beads on fabric following an existing pattern or design your own. You can use traditional embroidery stitches or make up ones as you go along. The choice is up to you.

The following projects highlight a couple of ways to use beads on fabric.

MATERIALS LIST

24 blue aurora borealis (AB) 4mm faceted fire-polish beads

18 red aurora borealis (AB) 4mm faceted fire-polish beads

24 lavender aurora borealis (AB) 4mm faceted fire-polish beads

10 green aurora borealis (AB) 6mm x 12mm leaf beads

11 amber 4mm faceted rondelle beads

2 grams yellow luster size 11° seed beads

1 gram green aurora borealis (AB) size 14° seed beads

Size 10 or 12 beading needle

4lb. Fireline™ or other bead embroidery thread

Scissors

Straight pins

bead-embroidered shirt

The addition of beads greatly enhances the curved neckline of a purchased T-shirt. Change the colors of the beads given here to match your shirt. The amount of embellishment is up to you. Just remember to allow a little stretch room in between the embroidered motifs.

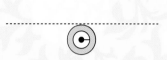

FIGURE 7–1

FIGURE 7–2

FIGURE 7–3

making the large flowers

1 Fold the shirt so the shoulder seams meet at the top of the shoulders. Mark the center front of the neckline with a straight pin. Lay the shirt out flat.

2 Cut about 1 yard (1m) of thread and single-thread the needle. Work the thread into the inside of the garment close to a seam so the stitching doesn't show from the front.

3 Starting about ½" (13mm) below the edge of the neckline in the center front, bring the needle to the front and pick up a rondelle bead and a yellow seed. Skip the yellow seed and pass back through the rondelle. Tack in place again with a tiny stitch on the inside of the garment (Figure 7–1).

4 Referring to Figure 7-2, bring the needle through to the front a short space away from the rondelle bead. Pick up 1 red fire-polish bead and lay it against the garment. Pass the needle back into the fabric at the other end of the bead. Pull the thread through and pull snug.

5 On the wrong side of the shirt, pass to the other side of the rondelle bead and stitch another red fire-polish bead in place as shown in Figure 7–3.

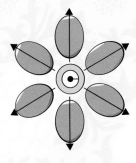

FIGURE 7–4

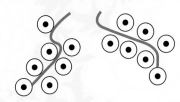

FIGURE 7–5

6 Sew 2 red fire-polish beads on either side of the 2 vertical beads as shown in Figure 7–4; make sure they are equally spaced apart and at an angle so it looks as if you have 6 petals on your flower.

7 Move right 5/8" (16mm) from the center flower and repeat Steps 3–6 with the lavender beads. Place this flower slightly above the 1st one. Refer to the photo on page 83 for placement.

8 When you have completed that flower, sew a blue one about 5/8" (16mm) further right; adjust it so it's not on the same level as the first 2.

9 Complete the large flowers on the right side by adding another red, lavender and blue flower, changing the positions slightly so they are not in a line.

10 Starting from the center for the left side, add blue, lavender, red, blue and lavender flowers in that order.

adding the leaves

1 Sew the leaves randomly in between the flowers.

2 Pass through the leaves several times to reinforce the stitching.

3 Place some leaf beads with the AB coating up and some down to vary the colors.

adding the tiny flowers

1 Do the baby's breath-type flowers by stitching the stems first.

2 Refer to the instructions for backstitching on pages 64–65 of the *Flower Basket Brooch*.

3 Backstitch random stems with the size 14 green seeds using 3–4 beads per stitch. Make them bend and twist as real stems do.

4 Randomly add the tiny flowers by stitching the size 11° yellow seeds offset on either side of the stems and at the very end. Refer to Figure 7–5 and the photo on page 83 for placement.

white daisies neck piece

A friend sent me these vintage white 2-hole nail heads; from the moment I opened the box, all I could think was "daisies."

This piece combines stringing with embroidery and vintage with new. With the raggedy green embroidered leaves and eyes made of yellow Charlottes, this piece will always make you feel it's summer.

TRANSFERRING THE PATTERN

Photocopy or scan the pattern on this page. Using white transfer paper and a stylus or empty ballpoint pen, go over key lines to transfer the design to the suede. Use as few marks as possible so they won't show when the embroidery is done. For instance, mark simple, short straight lines for the daisy petals and only the stems for the leaves.

If you feel comfortable with sketching, mark a minimal representation of the design on the suede using a white (removable) pencil. You could also use straight pins to mark select elements of the design for placement.

instructions

making the daisies

1 Single-thread the needle with 1 yard (1m) of 10 lb. white braided filament.

2 Pick up 15 of the white nail heads through 1 hole, making sure the faceted tops all face the same direction.

3 Gather up the thread and tie it into a secure double knot. Work the thread tails into the ring of beads and trim the excess threads. Set aside.

4 Repeat Step 2–3 twice more, but reduce the number of nail heads to 13 each. Set aside.

5 Transfer the pattern (Figure 7–6) onto the suede; see *Transferring the Pattern* on this page for suggested methods.

6 Arrange the center daisy on the piece of suede where shown on the pattern, making sure it maintains a round shape.

FIGURE 7–6

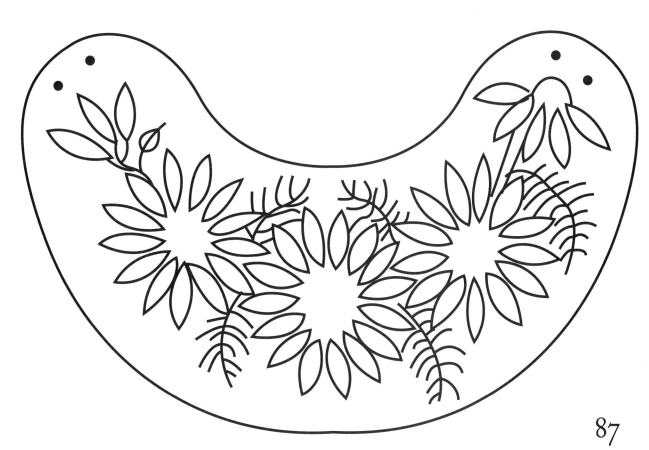

attaching the daisies in place

1 Thread the needle with 4lb. white thread and tie a knot in the very end.

2 Come up from the underside of the fabric between 2 of the nail heads along 1 side of the ring of connecting thread.

3 Pass the new thread over the ring of connecting thread and down through the fabric on the other side of the ring. Pull the thread through snugly.

4 Repeat Steps 2–3 between every nail head. This is called *couching* the beads in place.

5 When you have couched the thread between every bead, pass the needle to the underside of the fabric. Come up along a nail head and pass the needle through the 2nd hole in the bead and back into the fabric along the other side of the bead. Repeat all around the ring of beads. Tie off the thread.

6 Repeat all steps for the other 2 daisies.

7 On the upper left end of the piece, sew 3 nail heads in place using the couching method in Step 5.

8 Repeat for the half opened flower on the upper right end, attaching 5 nail heads using the method in Step 5.

sewing the eyes in place

1 The centers of the daisies are loops of yellow Charlottes. In the center of the largest daisy, bring a new 4lb. white thread through from the underside. Pick up 7 yellow beads and pass the needle back into fabric in almost the same hole.

2 Repeat Step 1 in a ring around the center loop, using about 5 loops.

3 Repeat Step 1 until you get to the nail heads, but use 5 beads per loop. Fill in the center area completely.

4 For the 2 smaller daisies, use loops of only 5 yellow beads.

5 For the half-open flower, use loops of 3 yellow beads.

embroidering the leaves

1 Following the pattern, backstitch the stems and center veins of the leaves in place (see pages 64–65 of *Flower Basket Brooch* for backstitching instructions). Use the 4lb. black thread and about 3 beads at a time.

2 Backstitch the sides of the leaves in place, varying the lengths of the rows so they look ragged.

CLOSE-UP OF DAISIES AND LEAVES

Note where the necklace beads connect to the suede.

completing the embroidery

1   Place a thin layer of fabric glue on the underside of the embroidered piece.

2   Place the 2 pieces of suede together so edges match and the glue is inside. Let dry thoroughly.

3   Follow the pattern to trim away excess suede, or trim and shape to suit yourself.

4   Single-thread the needle with about 2 yards (2m) of 4lb. black line. Tie a knot on the very end.

5   Bury the knot between the 2 layers of suede and weave a picot edge around the piece following the instructions in the *Flower Basket Brooch* project for doing a picot edge (page 86). Use the large black matte seeds for the base beads and the smaller black shiny beads for the point beads.

6   Work the threads into the piece. Knot and trim excess thread.

making the necklace

1   Cut 30" (76cm) of the 10 lb. black filament and thread a needle on each end.

2   On 1 needle, thread on 1 black matte seed and 1 black fire-polish bead twice, plus 1 more black matte seed. Center the beads.

3   Bring each needle through from the underside of the embroidered neck piece at 1 end. Refer to the photo on page 88 for placement.

4   Thread 1 black matte seed and 1 black fire-polish bead 3 times, plus 1 black matte seed on the lower needle.

5   Thread 1 black matte seed and 1 fire-polish bead twice on the upper needle.

6   Pass each needle through a nail head with the faceted side facing up.

7   On each needle, pick up 1 black matte seed, 1 black fire-polish bead and 1 black matte seed. Pass through the next nail head.

8   Repeat Step 7 until you have 15 nail heads or the length you want.

9   Pick up 1 black matte seed, 1 fire-polish bead and 1 black seed on 1 needle and pass through the shank of the black glass button.

10   Repeat Step 9 with the other needle.

11   Work the threads into the necklace, tying half hitch knots as you proceed.

12   Glue the knot and trim the excess thread ends.

13   Repeat Steps 1–8 on the other side of the necklace.

14   When you get to the last nail head, pick up 1 black matte seed, 1 fire-polish bead and 1 black seed on each needle.

15   On 1 needle pick up enough seeds to pass easily around the button.

16   Pass the other needle through the loop.

17   Repeat Steps 11–12.

Beading with Non-Beads

The subject matter of the first long book I wrote (*Beaded Jewelry with Found Objects*, Krause Publications, 2004) was using things not commonly found in beaded jewelry. There are projects made with drawer knobs, music box keys, copper pipe fittings and even rubber fishing worms. You can find inspiration for jewelry in some very unusual places. Just look around your world.

That's what this section is about—finding inspiration in items not normally used for jewelry.

MATERIALS LIST

5 assorted porcelain washer shapes, 20mm–24mm

One 24mm × 27mm porcelain flat spiral bead

One 14mm porcelain cube bead

Four 20mm (½") copper electrical washers

Three 16mm (⅜") copper electrical washers

Three 14mm (¼") copper electrical washers

One 24"(61cm) antique copper chain with 8mm links

Four 19mm decorative copper rings

Four 21mm × 9mm copper oval rings

Three 11mm copper spiral beads

Four 4mm × 6mm copper rondelle beads

Two 4mm round copper beads

Nine 2" (5cm) copper eye pins

Eight 9mm antique copper jump rings

One 12mm antique copper toggle clasp

1 pair antique copper ear wires

Chasing hammer

Steel block or anvil

Round nose pliers

Chain nose pliers

Wire cutters

off center jewelery set

At one of the largest bead shows in the United States, I met the owners of Off Center Productions (see *Resources*, page 140) who manufacture porcelain pendants, buttons and cabochons. Because of my interest in working with the unusual, I immediately was drawn to their products. This necklace is the marriage of their porcelain pieces, copper washers, vintage chain and copper beads, although you can substitute whatever you find.

instructions

texturing the washers

1 Place the steel block on a hard surface.

2 Using the ball end of the chasing hammer, beat each side of 1 copper washer to texture it. Be careful to keep your fingers out of the way.

3 Repeat for all copper washers. Set aside.

making the chain

1 Carefully open 1 end link of the chain and place the loop end of the toggle on it; close the link.

2 Count down 27 links and open the final link. Remove the rest of the chain.

3 Place a 14mm copper washer in the 27th link and close the link.

4 Remove 5 links from the larger piece of chain.

5 Place 1 end link around the small washer. Close the link.

6 Place the other end of the 5-link piece around a 16mm copper washer and close the link.

7 Repeat Step 4.

8 Place 1 end link around the 16mm washer from Step 6.

9 Place the remaining end link around a 20mm washer; close the link.

10 Remove 7 links of chain from the larger piece.

11 Attach 1 end to the washer from Step 9.

12 Repeat Steps 1–9 in reverse order for the other half of the neck chain; be sure to put the bar end of the toggle in place of the loop end. Set aside.

FIGURE 8–1

FIGURE 8–2

making the 9 dangles

1 Pass an eye pin through the center of 1 of the porcelain washers. Make a loop on the other end and bend the pin in half around the washer. Repeat for all remaining porcelain washers.

2 Re-move 4 links from the piece of chain and attach 1 link to a 16mm washer and the other end to the eye pin used in Step 1 (refer to Figure 8–1). Set aside.

3 For the 2nd dangle, refer to Figure 8–2; hook 1 of the decorative copper rings to 3 links of chain. Set aside.

FIGURE 8–3

FIGURE 8–4

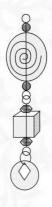

FIGURE 8–5

4 Thread a copper spiral bead on an eye pin. Trim the pin to 1" (25cm) and turn a spiral below the bead to hold it in place. Attach a pin to a porcelain washer from Step 1 with a link of chain (Figure 8–3.)

5 To make the 4th dangle, refer to Figure 8–4 and place a copper rondelle on one of the large jump rings. Attach the jump ring to one of the oval decorated rings. Place another jump ring on the other end.

6 To make the center dangle, refer to Figure 8–5. Thread a 4mm copper bead on an eye pin, then thread on the large porcelain spiral and another 4mm round bead. Turn a loop on the other end of the eye pin.

7 On a 2nd eye pin, thread on 1 rondelle, the porcelain cube bead and another rondelle. Turn a loop on the bottom of the pin. Attach this pin to the 1st one (Figure 8–5).

8 Hook a porcelain washer to the bottom of the 2nd eye pin with a jump ring (Figure 8–5). Set aside.

93

FIGURE 8–6

FIGURE 8–7

9   For the 6th dangle, attach a decorative copper ring to a spiral copper bead on an eye pin with a link of chain (Figure 8–6).

10   Refer to Figure 8–7 to make the 7th dangle. Attach 4 links of the chain to 1 of the porcelain washers. Attach a 14mm washer to the last link of the chain.

FIGURE 8–8

FIGURE 8–9

11   For the 8th dangle, connect an oval decorative ring to 1 link of chain and a jump ring (Figure 8–8).

12   For the 9th dangle, thread a spiral bead and a rondelle on an eye pin with a spiral turned on the bottom. Attach the pin to the last porcelain washer with 3 links of chain (Figure 8–9).

attaching the dangles

1   Starting on the left side of the necklace, attach Dangle 1 with a jump ring to the chain, 2 links to the right of the 14mm washer.

2   Attach Dangle 2 with a chain link to the 16mm washer.

3   Attach Dangle 3 with a jump ring to the chain, 2 links to the right of the 16mm washer.

4   Attach Dangle 4 with a chain link to the 20mm washer.

5   Attach the center dangle to the center link of the necklace.

6   Attach Dangle 6 with a chain link to the next 20mm washer.

7   Attach Dangle 7 to the chain, 4 links to the right of the 20mm washer.

8   Attach Dangle 8 with a jump ring to the 16mm washer.

9   Attach Dangle 9 (the final dangle) to the chain, 4 links to the right of the 16mm washer.

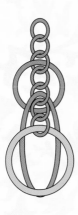

FIGURE 8–10

making the earrings

1 Refer to Figure 8–10 and cut a 7-link piece of chain.

2 Attach a round decorative ring to the 3rd link of the chain.

3 Attach an oval decorative link to the 5th link of the chain.

4 Attach a 20mm washer to the last link of the chain.

5 Attach the top link to 1 of the ear wires.

6 Repeat Steps 1–5 for the 2nd earring.

FISHING SPINNERS NECKLACE

Neon fishing spinners add flash and color to this bead and chain necklace. The fishing tackle store is a good place to look for non-bead items to use in jewelry.

95

MATERIALS LIST

Six $^{13}/_{16}$" (20mm)
black retaining rings

Two $^{7}/_{16}$" (11mm)
black retaining rings

Seven 11mm copper
spiral beads

Three 11mm × 10mm
fan-shaped beads

14 gun-metal gray 4mm
round metal beads

Three 3mm round
fluted copper beads

Seventeen 2mm
round copper beads

18" (46cm) copper
chain with 9mm links

Forty-four 6mm
copper jump rings

Ten 2" (5cm) copper
head pins

1 pair copper ear wires

One 12mm copper
toggle clasp

Chain nose pliers

Round nose pliers

Wire cutters

snap ring jewelry set

Snap or retaining rings normally are used on machinery, but in this necklace they make up the pendant. With the curved shape and the holes at the top, these serve as great jewelry components. They also come in a wide variety of sizes.

Check out your local parts store for more jewelry ideas.

FIGURE 8–11

FIGURE 8–12

making the pendant

1 Refer to Figure 8–11 and thread one 2mm copper bead, 1 gun-metal bead, 1 spiral bead, 1 gun-metal bead and one 2mm copper bead onto a head pin. Turn a loop and make a wrapped head pin. Repeat 6 more times. This creates Pin #1.

2 Refer to Figure 8–12 and thread one 2mm copper bead, 1 fan-shaped bead and one 3mm fluted copper bead on a head pin. Turn a loop and make a wrapped head pin. Repeat twice more. This creates Pin #2.

FIGURE 8–13

FIGURE 8–14

3 Attach two #2 pins and one #1 pin to a large snap ring. See Figure 8–13 for placement.

4 Attach 1 snap ring to either side of the one from the previous step. Use a jump ring through the hole in the snap ring and around the new one (Figure 8–14).

FIGURE 8–15

5 Attach a #1 pin on each side snap ring as shown in Figure 8–14 on page 97.

6 Attach 3 snap rings across the top as shown in Figure 8–15. Attach a #2 pin to the center ring.

making the necklace

1 Make sure the necklace chain has an uneven number of links.

2 Attach the loop end of the toggle to the chain with a jump ring.

3 Attach the bar end of the toggle to the chain with 3 jump rings.

FIGURE 8–16

attaching the pendant to the necklace

1 Hook a jump ring in each hole at the top of the pendant.

2 Find the center link of the chain. Place a jump ring in every other link on either side of the center link until you have 3 jump rings on either side.

3 Attach the pendant jump rings to the jump rings on the chain with a 3rd set of jump rings.

making the earrings

1 Refer to Figure 8–16 and attach one #1 pin to a small snap ring as shown.

2 Place a jump ring in each hole of the snap ring.

3 Hook both jump rings to the ear wire with a 3rd jump ring.

4 Repeat Steps 1–3 for the 2nd earring.

Fun With Findings

Findings are those things you usually need to make or finish a piece of jewelry—jump rings, clasps, strand connectors, etc. Findings rarely get to be the jewelry itself.

That's where the following projects vary from normal; they put the focus on the finding. You may never look at findings the same way again.

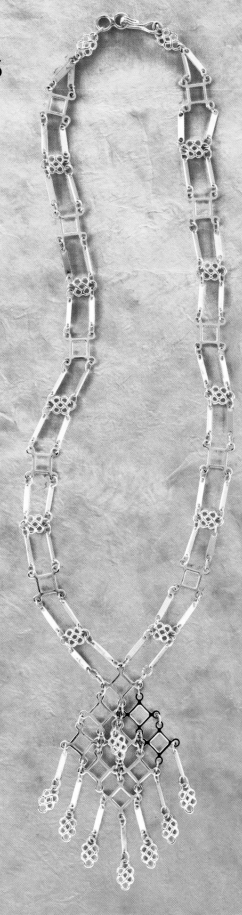

MATERIALS LIST

3 gold-colored 25mm
jump rings (A)

8 gold-colored 17mm
jump rings (B)

66 gold-colored 9mm
jump rings (C)

29 red 9mm glass
rings (D)

22 pink 9mm
glass rings (E)

1 pair gold ball, loop
and post earrings

1 gold lobster claw clasp

Chain nose pliers

brass & glass rings set

The focus of this project is the jump ring. In fact, the entire project is constructed of jump rings and glass rings. It's an easy project to do, although you may get tired of opening and closing jump rings.

Here's a tip: Use one of those jump ring opener/closer tools that fit over your finger. It looks like a ring with grooves in it. You fit the jump ring into the groove and twist to open or close. This tool will make this project a lot easier.

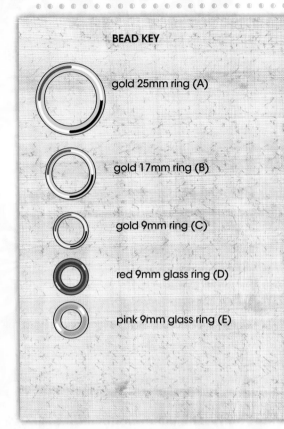

instructions

BEAD KEY

gold 25mm ring (A)

gold 17mm ring (B)

gold 9mm ring (C)

red 9mm glass ring (D)

pink 9mm glass ring (E)

FIGURE 9–1

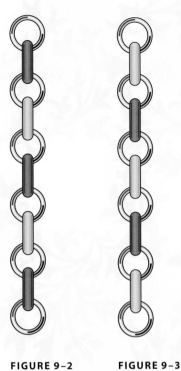

FIGURE 9–2　　　**FIGURE 9–3**

making the chains

1　Attach a small jump ring (C) to a red glass ring (D). Add a 2nd jump ring (C) and a pink glass ring (E).

2　Repeat Step 1. End this piece of chain with a small jump ring (C), a red ring (D) and a small jump ring (C). Your chain should be (C), (D), (C), (E), (C), (D), (C), (E), (C), (D) and (C) (Figure 9-2).

3　Make 3 more of these chains for a total of 4. Set them aside.

4　Refer to Figure 9–3 and make 2 chains as follows: (C), (E), (C), (D), (C), (E), (C), (D), (C), (E) and (C).

FIGURE 9–4

making the pendants

1　Place 1 small jump ring (C) through each of 3 red rings (D) and through each of 2 pink rings (E).

2　Attach the jump rings (C) to a large jump ring (A) in the following manner: red, pink, red, pink and red (Figure 9–4).

3　Repeat Steps 1–2 twice more with the other 2 large rings (A).

IOI

FIGURE 9–5

assembling the necklace

1 Attach the 3 pendant rings together with a small jump ring (C) as shown in Figure 9–5.

2 Attach 1 end of the 3-ring pendant to a medium jump ring (B) with a small jump ring (C) as shown in Figure 9–5.

3 Add 1 of the chains from Figure 9–2 on page 101 (one that starts with a red ring) with the end jump ring of the chain. Refer to Figure 9–5 and to the photo on page 100.

4 Attach the end jump ring of the chain to a medium jump ring (B).

5 Attach the end jump ring of a chain from Figure 9–3 on page 101 (one that starts with a pink ring) to the medium jump ring you just added.

6 Attach the other end of the pink chain to another medium jump ring (B) with the end jump ring in the chain.

7 Add a 2nd chain that starts with a red ring to the (B) ring.

8 The final step for that side of the necklace is to add the lobster claw clasp in the last jump ring of the 2nd red chain.

9 Repeat Steps 2–8 for the other side of the necklace.

10 Add an extra small jump ring (C) in the end ring of the last chain.

FIGURE 9–6

making the earrings

1 Place 1 small jump ring (C) through each of 4 red rings (D) and through each of 2 pink rings (E).

2 Attach 1 red, 1 pink, and 1 red glass ring/jump ring sets to a medium jump ring (B).

3 Attach a small jump ring (C) to a larger ring (A) (Figure 9–6).

4 Attach a smaller ring (C) to the earring finding.

5 Repeat Steps 2–4 for the other earring.

MATERIALS LIST

19 silver 4-hole
connectors (A)

20 oval filigree silver
connectors (B)

51 silver 11mm
2-hole strand spacers
(C) (Beadalon®)

122 silver 4mm jump
rings (D) (Beadalon®)

6 silver 4mm ×
5mm jump rings
(E) (Beadalon®)

1 wire hook and
eye for clasp

Chain nose pliers

Bead sorting
dish or cloth

four-hole connectors pendant

To me, these four-hole connectors just scream possibilities. Their shape is reminiscent of the pattern in right- angle weave, which lends itself to weaving fabric-like pieces. The oval connectors were a must-have as well.

Combined with two-hole strand separators and joined with jump rings, this necklace is made entirely of findings. Beading is no longer just for the beads.

BEAD KEY

4-hole connector (A)

Oval filigree connector (B)

2-hole strand spacer (C)

4mm jump ring (D)

4mm x 5mm jump ring (E)

FIGURE 9–7

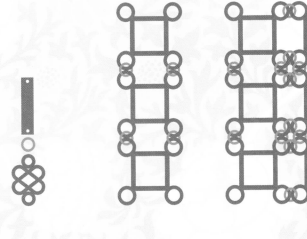

FIGURE 9–8   **FIGURE 9–9**   **FIGURE 9–10**

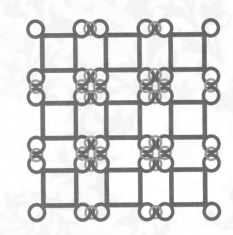

FIGURE 9–11

making the pendant

1 Refer to the Bead Key (Figure 9–7). Make 7 dangles by attaching 1 oval filigree connector (B) to one 11mm 2-hole strand spacer (C) with a 4mm jump ring (D) (Figure 9–8). Set aside.

2 Hook two 4-hole connectors (A) together on 2 holes as shown in Figure 9–9 with a 4mm jump ring (D). Repeat for a 3rd connector, making 3 in a row. Repeat twice more, making 3 strips of 3.

3 Attach two 4-hole connector strips together (Figure 9–10) with 4mm jump rings (D).

4 Attach a 3rd 4-hole connector strip in the same manner as in Step 3 (Figure 9–11).

FIGURE 9–12

FIGURE 9–13

making the chain

5 Turn the square of connectors on the diagonal. Attach a dangle from Step 1 to the upper hole of each 4-hole connector (A) with a 4mm jump ring (D) as shown in Figure 9–12.

6 Attach a filigree connector (B) just above the center connector with two 4mm jump rings (D) as seen in Figure 9–12. Set aside while you make the chain.

1 Attach a filigree connector (B) with two 2-hole strand spacers (C) using a 4mm jump ring (D) (Figure 9–13).

2 Refer to Figure 9–14 (page 107) for the following:
 Attach a 4-hole connector (A) to the 2-hole strand spacers (C).
 Now attach a 2-hole strand spacer (C) to each bottom hole of the 4-hole connector (A) with a 4mm jump ring (D).
 Turn a filigree connector (B) sideways and attach to the strand spacers (C).
 Add 2 more 2-hole strand spacers (C).

3 Repeat Step 2 completely (from the red dotted line marked *A* on Figure 9–14, page 107) until you have added 4 more patterns.

4 Repeat Steps 1–3 for the other side of the necklace.

5 Place half of the clasp on the beginning end of the chain through the filigree connector (B). Use 1 of the 4mm × 5mm jump rings (E) .

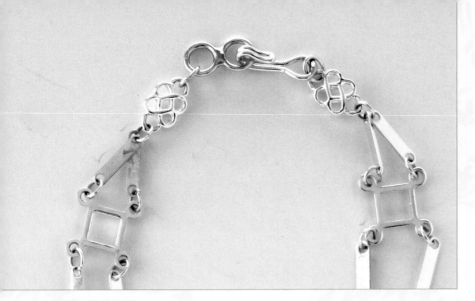

DETAIL OF CLASP

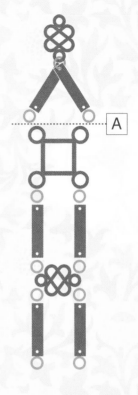

FIGURE 9–14

adding the pendant

1 Lay the pendant and chains out on your work surface. Line them up so everything lies correctly.

2 Using a 4mm jump ring (D), attach the inside 2-hole spacer (C) to the top center hole of the pendant (see photo on page 104).

3 Hook one 4 × 5mm oval jump ring (E) through the 2-hole spacer (C) on 1 side of the necklace and close. See Figure 9–12 (page 106) for placement at the orange arrows.

4 Hook the 2nd 4mm × 5mm jump ring (E) into the side hole of the top of the pendant and into the one you just put into the strand spacer (C). Close. See Figure 9–12 (page 106) for placement at the orange arrows.

5 Repeat Steps 2–4 for the other side of the necklace.

Using Multiple-Hole Beads

Occasionally you will find beads that have more than one hole in them. Such beads offer the adventurous beading enthusiast a unique opportunity to do things not possible with one-hole beads, especially in the area of bead weaving.

Most of the two-hole beads you will find today are vintage, but new ones are being made. Watch for them —perhaps you can use the ideas presented in these projects to make something exciting with them.

MATERIALS LIST

8 lavender 16mm
x 20mm 2-hole
flower beads

7 purple 4mm
bicone crystals
(wildthingsbeads.com)

222 white pearl size
11° seed beads

1 silver 12mm
magnetic clasp

4 silver clamshell
bead tips

Four 2mm crimp beads

2 yards (2m) .011"
(.28mm) diameter white
beading thread or
8 lb. braided filament
(DandyLine™ was
used in this project)

Size 10 or 12
beading needle

Round nose pliers

Blade scissors

Glue (Gem-Tac™ was
used in this project)

lavender flowers bracelet

The lavender flower beads in this bracelet are reproductions of old beads. This is one of those projects that didn't come out the way I planned the first time around. Sometimes you have to make adjustments as you bead.

Length: 8" (20cm)

instructions

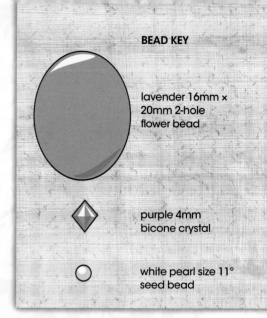

BEAD KEY

lavender 16mm x 20mm 2-hole flower bead

purple 4mm bicone crystal

white pearl size 11° seed bead

FIGURE 10-1

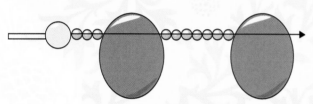

FIGURE 10-2

FIGURE 10-3

making the straight path

1 Single-thread a needle with about 18" (46cm) of thread.

2 Tie a crimp securely on the end, leaving a tail of about 4" (10cm).

3 Pass the thread through the clamshell from the inside out. Do not close the clamshell. Leave the thread tail hanging loose.

4 Pick up 3 seeds (Figure 10–2).

5 Refer to Figure 10–2 and pass through 1 hole of 1 of the flower beads.

6 Pick up 7 seeds.

7 Pass into the next flower bead (Figure 10–2).

8 Continue repeating Steps 6–7 until you have all 8 flower beads threaded on.

9 Pick up 3 seeds on the other end and pass into a clamshell bead from the bottom up.

10 Pull the beads up snug. Tie on a crimp. Remove the needle and let the thread tail hang.

11 Repeat Steps 1–10 for the bottom row as shown in Figure 10-3.

making the crosses

1 Single-thread a needle with about 18" (46cm) of thread.

2 Tie the thread into the crimp inside the top clamshell bead tip leaving a 4" (10cm) tail.

3 Pass through the clamshell, the first 3 seeds and the 1st flower bead.

4 Pick up 4 seeds, a bicone crystal and 4 seeds.

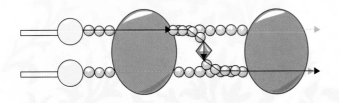

FIGURE 10-4

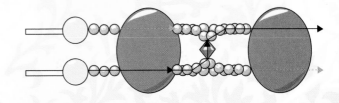

FIGURE 10-5

5 Pass diagonally across to and through the bottom hole of the next flower bead (Figure 10–4).

6 Repeat Steps 4–5 across the bracelet. If you come out of the bottom hole of 1 flower bead, go diagonally across to the top hole on the next one. Keep reversing holes as you move across the bracelet.

7 Pass through the last flower bead, the 3 seeds and the clamshell bead tip.

8 Pull the beads up snug. Tie the thread around the crimp. Remove the needle and let the thread hang.

9 Repeat Steps 1–2.

10 Pass through the clamshell the first 3 seeds and the 1st flower bead in the bottom hole (the one you didn't use the 1st time).

11 Pick up 4 seeds.

12 Pass through the crystal from the strand shown in Figure 10–4.

13 Pick up 4 more seeds and pass into the top hole in the next flower bead (the one you didn't use the 1st time). Refer to Figure 10–5.

14 Repeat Steps 6–8.

finishing the bracelet

1 You should have 2 threads coming out of each clamshell. Tie off the threads against the clamshell.

2 Trim the thread ends, glue the knot and close the clamshell.

3 Repeat for the remaining clamshells.

4 With round nose pliers, bend the bar of 1 clamshell around 1 of the loops in the clasp.

5 Repeat for other 3 clamshells and loops.

MATERIALS LIST

60 square 9mm 2-hole beads (holes diagonal through the corners)

5 grams pink luster size 11° seed beads

1 silver 12mm toggle clasp

1 pair silver ball, loop and post earrings

5 silver 4mm jump rings

4 silver clamshell bead tips

Four 2mm crimp beads

5 yds 6 lb. crystal Fireline™

2 size 10 beading needles

Glue

Blade scissors

Chain nose pliers

Round nose pliers

Bead sorting dish or cloth

pink squares jewelry set

This necklace is woven with square two-hole beads in ladder stitch. This stitch is similar to right-angle weave. Check *Beading Basics* (Krause Publications, 2006) for more information on ladder stitch.

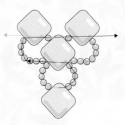

making the pendant

1 Cut a length of thread about 2 yards (2m) long; place a needle on each end of it.

2 Pick up a square bead on 1 needle and center the bead on the thread.

3 Pick up 5 seeds on each needle.

FIGURE 10-6

4 Pass each needle through a 2nd square bead from opposite directions. Make sure that you have the rounded sides up on both of the square beads and that you are passing through the upper hole of the 1st bead and the lower hole of the top bead (Figure 10-6).

5 The needles should be coming out of the 2nd square bead pointing away from the beads. On the right-hand needle, pick up 7 seeds, 1 square bead and 1 seed.

FIGURE 10-7

6 Pass through the top hole of the 2nd square bead as shown in Figure 10-7, through another seed and through a 4th square bead. Pull the thread snug.

7 With the left-hand needle, pick up 7 seeds and pass through the 4th square bead, the seed, the 3rd square bead and the seed as shown in Figure 10-7. Pull the thread snug.

FIGURE 10-8

8 For the next row, on the right-hand needle pick up 7 seeds, the 5th square bead, 1 seed, the 6th square bead, 1 seed and the 7th square bead (Figure 10-8).

9 Thread 7 seeds on the left-hand needle and pass through the 7th square bead, the seed, the 6th square bead, the seed and the 5th square bead. Pull the thread snug (Figure 10-8).

10 Do the next 3 rows in the same manner, except add 1 additional square bead to each row (as shown in the photo on page 112) so the last row has 6 square beads across the top.

11 When you complete the last row, your threads will be coming out of opposite sides of the pendant. On the right-hand needle, pick up 7 seeds and pass thorough the top hole of the end bead (the 17th square).

12 Pick up 6 seeds and pass through the top hole of the next bead. Repeat this step until you have passed across the top of the beads.

13 On the left-hand needle, pick up 7 seeds; pass through all of the beads at the top of the piece that you just passed through with the right-hand needle.

14 Work the thread tails into the work, tying half hitch knots as you proceed. Be sure to follow the pattern so no thread shows. Trim the excess thread ends close to the work.

DOUBLE DAGGERS NECKLACE

This necklace features a large lamp-worked bead by artist Tanya McGuire. The dagger beads have two holes which allow for the interesting combination of large and small beads in the necklace.

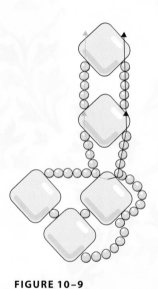

FIGURE 10–9

adding the necklace

1 Cut 1 yard (1m) of thread and place a needle on each end.

2 Refer to Figure 10–9. Pass 1 needle through the top of the 17th bead, which is in the upper right corner of the pendant. Center the thread.

3 Pick up 5 seeds on each needle.

4 Pass each needle through 1 hole on a square bead, being sure the rounded side is the same as the pendant (Figure 10–9).

5 Repeat Steps 3–4 until you have added 17 square beads or completed the length you want.

6 Pick up 5 seeds on each needle.

7 Pass each needle through 1 seed to end the strand. Loosely tie off.

8 Repeat Steps 1–7 for the other side of the necklace.

finishing the necklace

1 Untie 1 end of the necklace and pass the threads through a clamshell bead tip from the bottom up.

2 Pass 1 thread through a crimp.

3 Tie off the threads against the crimp. Glue the knot and trim the thread tails. Close the clamshell.

4 Bend the bar of the clamshell into a loop and pass around the loop end of the toggle.

5 Repeat Steps 1–3 for the other side of the necklace.

6 Hook 3 of the jump rings together, putting the end one around the bar end of the toggle.

7 Bend the bar end of the clamshell into a loop and around the other end of the 3 jump rings.

FIGURE 10–10

making the earrings

1 Cut a length of thread about 12" (30cm) long; place a needle on each end.

2 Pick up a square bead and center it on the thread (Figure 10–10).

3 On each needle, pick up 5 seeds.

4 Pass through the bottom hole of a 2nd square bead.

5 Pick up 7 seeds on each needle; pass each needle through the remaining hole in the 2nd square bead from opposite directions.

6 Pick up 5 seeds on each needle. Pass both needles through 1 last seed.

7 Pass both needles through a clamshell bead tip from the bottom up.

8 Pass 1 needle through a crimp.

9 Tie off the threads against the crimp. Glue the knot and trim the thread ends. Close the clamshell.

10 Bend the bar end of a clamshell into a loop and attach it with a jump ring to an earring finding.

11 Repeat Steps 1–10 for the 2nd earring.

section three:
experimenting & exploring

If you have worked your way through the book, you should be ready for this section. The projects in this final section may look difficult, but they are really just a combination of stitches or techniques you learned earlier.

Interesting projects can be made by combining stitches and patterns. Many of the projects I've had published over the years came about through experimenting with ways to change or improve upon existing techniques. Sometimes, a very simple adjustment can make a pattern into something quite different looking. *Right Angles & Ladders Bracelet* (page 123) and the neck strap on *Aurichalcite Necklace* (page 134) are actually the same basic weave. The addition of the drop beads in the bracelet makes the two projects look entirely different.

Earlier in my career, I was a silversmith and used gemstone cabochons to make silver and gold jewelry. I started beading many years after I quit metal work, but I still had a number of cabochons left over. On a trip to Arizona, I saw my first beaded cabochon and I immediately had to try one. The beaded cabochons in the projects in this section are done using the same technique I learned from beaders in Arizona—the leather-backed method, which combines glue, back-stitch, peyote stitch, couching and simple stringing to hold the cabochons in place.

A beaded cabochon can be a time-consuming project, but well worth the effort. For several other methods of beading around cabochons, see my book *Beaded Jewelry with Found Objects* (Krause Publications, 2004).

New Ways With Old Weaves

By starting with the basic steps you've learned in this book and others, you can begin to come up with patterns on your own. I came up with the bracelet patterns in this section while I was playing around with some old weaves to see how I might change or embellish the basic weave. Experimentation is a great way to learn. Save your mistakes—on another day, you might see how to use or change them to make them useful.

MATERIALS LIST

66 faceted 4mm
fire-polish (FP) beads

3 grams size 11°
seed beads

2 grams size 14°
seed beads

One ⅝" (16mm)
diameter shank button

4½ yds (4m)
6 lb. FireLine™

2 size 10 or 12
beading needles

Gem-Tac™ Permanent
Adhesive

Scissors

Bead sorting
dish or cloth

twin serpentine bracelet

Although nearly all of the work in this book is new, this project was first published in *Jewelry Crafts Magazine* and taught numerous times. It is one of my most popular classes and kits, and I wanted to share it with you here. The basic flat serpentine weave has been around for a while. The embellished version is an example of how you can use simple weaves in more complicated ways.

Length: 7" (18cm)

instructions

making the serpentine bands

1   Single-thread a needle with about 3½' (107cm) of thread.

2   Leaving a 12" (30cm) tail, pick up 6 size 11º seeds, 1 size 14º seed, 1 fire-polish (FP) bead and 1 size 14º seed (Figure 11–1).

3   Pass the needle back through the size 11º seeds in the same direction and pull up snug (Figure 11–2). You should have a loop as shown in Figure 11–3.

4   Pick up 4 size 11º seeds, 1 size 14º seed, 1 FP and 1 size 14º seed (Figure 11–4).

5   Pass the needle back through the last 2 size 11º seeds of the 1st pattern and the 4 size 11º seeds you just picked up (Figure 11–5). Pull up snug. Your piece should look like Figure 11–6.

6   Pick up 4 size 11º seeds, 1 size 14º seed, 1 FP and 1 size 14º seed (Figure 11–7). Pass the needle back through the last 2 size 11º seeds of the 2nd pattern and the 4 size 11º seeds you just picked up.

7   Continue in this manner until you have a band long enough to just meet around your wrist. Be sure to do an uneven number of patterns. Set the piece aside with the thread hanging.

8   Repeat Steps 1–7 for the 2nd band. Be sure the bands are the same length.

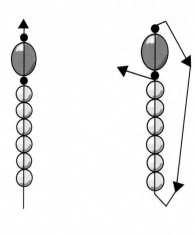

FIGURE 11–1   **FIGURE 11–2**

FIGURE 11–3   **FIGURE 11–4**

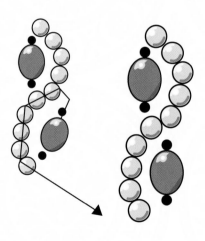

FIGURE 11–5   **FIGURE 11–6**

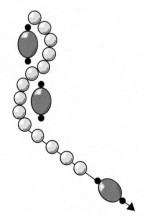

FIGURE 11–7

FIGURE 11–8

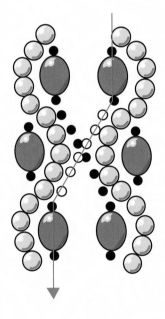

FIGURE 11–9

weaving bands together

1 Lay the 2 bands side by side in front of you; the sides of the bands with the most patterns (uneven sides) should be facing each other (Figure 11–8).

2 Single-thread a needle with 1 yard (1m) of thread. Tie on a waste bead, leaving a 12" (30cm) thread tail.

3 Pass the needle through the size 14 seed°, FP, size 14 seed° pattern on 1 band as shown in Figure 11–8.

4 Pick up 6 size 14° seeds.

5 Pass diagonally across to the 3rd pattern of the 2nd band. Pass through the size 14° seed, FP, size 14° seed pattern.

6 Pick up 6 size 14° seeds.

7 Pass back to the 1st band and through the 5th size 14° seed, FP, 14 seed° pattern.

8 Continue down the bands in this manner. Leave excess thread at other end and remove the needle.

9 Repeat the process starting on the other side of the band from Step 1 (Figure 11–9). The size 14° seeds should crisscross down the bands (refer to the photo on page 119).

FIGURE 11–10

FIGURE 11–11

finishing the bracelet

1 There should be 2 threads coming out of each side at each end of the bracelet. Insert 1 pair of threads from 1 end of the band into a needle. Repeat for the other set of threads at that end.

2 Pick up 2 size 11º seeds on 1 needle. Pass through the shank of the button. Pick up 2 size 11º seeds. Pass the needle into the size 11º seeds on the other side of the band (Figure 11–10).

3 Tie off the threads by tying some half hitch knots as you work through the size 11º seeds. Glue the knots and trim the excess thread.

4 Pass the 2nd needle through the 2 size 11º seeds, the shank of the button and 2 size 11º seeds. Bury the tails in the size 11º seeds on the other side of the band (Figure 11–10).

5 On the other end of bracelet, place the thread pairs into the needles. Pick up enough beads on 1 needle to pass easily over the button (Figure 11–11).

6 Bury and tie off the threads in size 11º seeds on the other side of the band. Glue the knots and trim the excess threads.

7 Pass the 2nd needle through the bead loop and bury the tails in size 11º seeds on the other side of the band (Figure 11–11). Glue the knots and trim the excess threads.

MATERIALS LIST

Seventy 4mm
drop beads

Thirty-six 4mm
bicone crystals

4 grams size 11°
shiny seed beads

2 grams size 11°
matte seed beads

One ⅝" (16mm) or
¾" (19mm) shank
button to match beads

3–4 yds (3–4m) beading
thread (Fireline™
or PowerPro™)

2 size 10 or 12
beading needles

Blade scissors

Bead sorting
dish or cloth

Gem glue

right angles & ladders bracelet

This bracelet came about when I was trying to figure out a new neck strap to use on the *Aurichalcite Necklace & Earrings* (page 134). If you do all the steps except add the drops in the last pass, you will have the pattern for the neck strap. The drops add a different dimension to the weave, making it more fun and flirty.

Length: 7" (18cm)

Note: *There are about five crystals per inch (13mm) of woven bracelet (plus one extra for the end) and ten drop beads per inch (13mm). Make a bracelet long enough to meet around your wrist with a little wiggle room.*

FIGURE 11–12

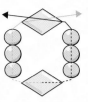

FIGURE 11–13

weaving the crystal band

1 Cut as much thread as you can handle (about 2½ yards [2m] should complete the bracelet without adding thread). Place a needle on each end of the thread and pull up so the ends are even in length.

2 Pick up 3 shiny seeds, 1 crystal and 3 shiny seeds (Figure 11–12). Center the beads on the thread.

3 Pick up another crystal on 1 needle. Pass the 2nd needle through the same crystal from the opposite direction (Figure 11–13). Pull up snug.

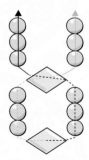

FIGURE 11–14

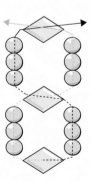

FIGURE 11–15

4 Pick up 3 shiny seeds on each needle as shown in Figure 11–14.

5 Pick up 1 crystal on 1 needle and pass through the crystal with the other needle in the opposite direction as seen in Figure 11–15. Pull up snug.

6 Repeat Steps 4 and 5 until you have the length you need, finishing with a crystal. Keep in mind that you must calculate your bracelet length based on the information given in the project introduction on page 123.

adding the button

1 Pick up 3 shiny seeds on each needle.

2 Pass 1 needle through the shank of the button (Figure 11–16).

3 Pass the needle around the last pattern of the bracelet, coming back out through the shank of the button.

4 Repeat with the other needle, passing through from the opposite direction.

5 Wrap the shank of the button several times with each thread to strengthen.

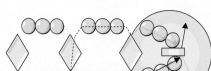

FIGURE 11–16

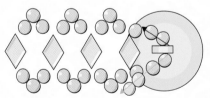

FIGURE 11–17

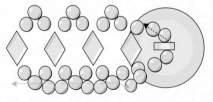

FIGURE 11–18

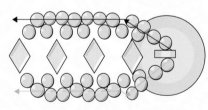

FIGURE 11–19

weaving in the matte beads

1 Pass 1 needle through the 2 seeds closest to the shank of the button (Figure 11–17).

2 Pick up 2 matte seeds as shown in Figure 11–17.

3 Pass through the center of the 3 shiny seeds you picked up when making the crystal band (Figure 11–18).

4 Continue picking up 2 matte seeds in between each of the shiny seeds as shown in Figure 11–18.

5 Continue to the other end of the band.

6 Repeat Steps 1–6 on other side of the band as shown in Figure 11–19.

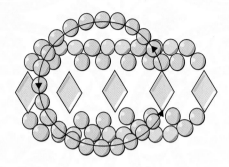

FIGURE 11–20

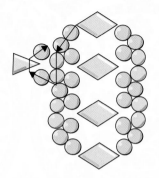

FIGURE 11–21

adding the loop

1 Work the threads back around the end of the bracelet and come out with a needle on either side of the 4th crystal from the end.

2 Pick up enough seeds on 1 needle to make a loop big enough to go around the button with a little ease room (Figure 11–20).

3 Pass around the bead loop with the other needle.

4 Work the threads back to the end of the bracelet.

adding the drops

1 Pass 1 thread through the 2 shiny seeds on the end of the band as shown in Figure 11–21.

2 Pass through the 2 matte seeds.

3 Pick up 1 shiny seed, 1 drop and 1 shiny seed.

4 Loop the thread around and back through the 2 matte seeds in the same direction you just went. Refer to Figure 11–21.

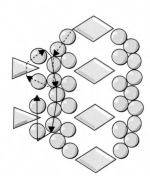

FIGURE 11-22

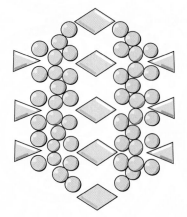

FIGURE 11-23

5 Pass through the next shiny seed and 2 matte seeds as shown in Figure 11–22.

6 Pick up 1 shiny seed, 1 drop and 1 shiny seed.

7 Loop the thread around and back through the 2 matte seeds in the same direction you just went (Figure 11–22).

8 Continue to the end of the band.

9 Repeat Steps 1–8 with the other needle (Figure 11–23).

finishing up

1 Work the thread tails into the work, tying several half hitch knots as you weave.

2 Glue the thread tails and trim the ends.

Combining Stitches

Once you have learned the basics of a number of stitches, you can combine them in a million different ways to make interesting new designs. Such is the case when you bead around cabochons.

Cabochons are usually made of gemstone, glass or other hard material. They have one flat side and one domed or faceted side. Cabochons come in calibrated sizes to fit premade settings, or they're free-form like the ones used here.

The instructions for these projects are guidelines only. Each application will require differing amounts of beads and supplies, but these general instructions will work on most any kind of flat-backed cabochon.

MATERIALS LIST

One 1½" × 2"
(4cm × 5cm) polymer
clay cabochon (River
Poet Designs)

3 grams black matte
size 11° seed beads

2 grams black size
14° seed beads

1 gram pumpkin size
11° seed beads

40 black 3mm
tube beads

32 black 4mm faceted
fire-polish beads

Two 3" × 4" (8cm x
10cm) pieces of black
synthetic suede

One 1¼" (32cm)
silver pin back

6 lb. black Fireline™

Size 10 beading needle

Size 10 sharps needle

Fabri-Tac™ Fabric Glue

Gem-Tac™ Permanent
Adhesive

Blade scissors

Bead sorting
dish or cloth

butterfly & flowers brooch

The centerpiece of this brooch is a thin, flat piece of polymer clay made by Lynne Ann Schwarzenberg of River Poet Designs; it is full of amazing detail and color. The piece is a complicated pattern, so a simple setting seemed in order. Several stitches are used in this project, but it's a good first beaded cabochon.

FIGURE 12–1

FIGURE 12–2

preparing the cabochon

1 Place a thin coat of gem glue on the back of the cabochon to within 1/16" (2mm) of the edge.

2 Center the cabochon on 1 piece of the suede. Place heavy books on top and let it sit overnight or until the glue is completely dry.

beading the bezel

1 A bezel is a band that goes around the stone to hold it in place. The bezel in this project is a band of peyote stitched beads. To begin, cut a piece of thread as long as you can handle. Single-thread the sharps needle with the thread and knot the end of the thread.

2 Bring the needle up from the underside of the suede about half a size 11° seed's width away from the cabochon along 1 of the longer sides of the piece. Pull the thread through until the knot is buried in the suede.

3 Pick up 3 black matte 11° beads and lay them along the cabochon as shown in Figure 12–1. Pass the needle back into the suede at the end of the beads and pull through to the underside.

4 Pass the needle back through the 1st hole you made and through the 3 beads again. Pick up 3 new beads and pass back through the suede—you are backstitching the beads in place around the cabochon. (For more information on backstitching, see the instructions for the *Flower Basket Brooch,* pages 62–66).

5 Bring the needle up from behind and through the 4th bead back from the end. Pass through the 4 beads and pick up 3 new beads. Pass back into the suede.

6 Repeat Step 3 until you have ringed the cabochon (Figure 12–2). Try to use an even number of beads in the ring, which will be the first 2 rows of the peyote band.

7 Pass the needle back through the ring again to reinforce it. Pass the needle through to the underside.

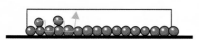

FIGURE 12–3

FIGURE 12–4

making the peyote band

1 Bring the needle up through the ring of beads and pass through 1 of them.

2 Pick up a black size 11° seed. Skip the next bead in the ring and pass through the 3rd one. Refer to Figure 12–3. Pull the thread through.

3 Pick up a 2nd black size 11° seed and pass through the 5th bead in the base ring (Figure 12–3).

4 Continue around the ring adding a new bead every other bead in the base ring (as shown in Figure 12–4) until you get back to the beginning.

5 The beads in the base row will move some as you work, making the band look more like peyote stitch as you develop the up-and-down pattern. (For more information on the peyote stitch, refer to pages 46–47.) The row you just finished is the 3rd row.

6 When you get back to the beginning, "step up" by passing the needle through the 1st bead you added in the 3rd row to start the 4th row.

FIGURE 12–5

FIGURE 12–6

7 Work a new bead between every bead from the last row. Pull snug (Figure 12–5).

8 Before you add the final row, determine if you need another row of size 11° beads to come up to the top edge of the cabochon. If so, add it or enough rows so that the beads come up to the top edge (or over the curve of the cabochon if you are using a domed one).

9 If you don't need another row of size 11° beads, make the final row with black size 14° seeds instead (Figure 12–6).

10 Pass through the final row of beads again to reinforce and pull as tightly as you can. Work the needle back to the underside through the bezel beads following the diagonal pattern of the beads. Tie off the thread.

FIGURE 12-7

FIGURE 12-8

adding the first row of embellishment

1 Start with a new thread and knot the end. Bring the needle up from the underside just to the side of the bezel along 1 long side.

2 Alternately pick up 1 black matte seed and one 3mm tube until you have enough to fit snugly around the bezel. Be sure to end with a tube.

3 See Figure 12-7. Lay the ring around the bezel and pass the needle back through the ring to reinforce (as shown in the orange dotted line). Pass back through to the underside and tie off, but do not cut the thread.

4 To "couch" the ring in place and keep the beads from "squirming" as you work, bring the needle up from the underside between the bezel and the ring of beads in the middle of 1 side. Pass the needle over the ring and down into the suede on the other side of the ring, passing over the thread in the ring of beads. Note the orange line across the ring in Figure 12-7. Pull the thread snug and it should disappear between 2 beads.

5 Pass to other side of the ring (on the underside) and repeat Step 4, noting the orange line in Figure 12-7.

6 Pass to the top center and repeat Step 4. Then pass to the bottom center and repeat Step 4.

7 Now repeat this step between every 2 beads all around the ring.

adding the second row of embellishment

1 The 2nd and final row of embellishment is a ring of black 4mm fire-polish beads alternating with a pumpkin size 11° seed.

2 As before, make the ring big enough to pass around the previous ring and fit snugly. Pass through the beads again to reinforce.

3 Couch the ring in place as you did in the previous row (Figure 12-8).

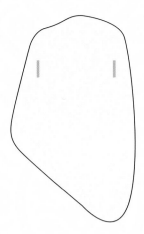

FIGURE 12–9

adding the backing

1 Trim the excess suede ¼" (6mm) away from the last row of beading. Later you will trim it closer.

2 Lay the brooch on the backing piece and cut the backing piece to match the shape of the brooch.

3 Refer to Figure 12–9. Determine where you want to position the pin back—it should be in the top third of the brooch to make the brooch hang correctly. Make a mark at either end of where the pin back should go, then make a small slit at each mark.

4 Place some glue on the bar of the pin back, then insert the pin back through the backing piece from the underside.

5 Glue the backing piece to the brooch with fabric glue; be sure to get the glue out to the edges. Allow the glue to dry thoroughly.

6 Trim the suede to within 1/16" (2mm) of the beading; be careful not to cut any of the threads that hold the beads in place.

adding the picot edge

1 Refer to the directions for making a picot edge in the *Flower Basket Brooch* instructions (page 66).

2 Use the black matte size 11º seeds for the base of the picot and the size 14º black beads for the point beads.

3 Do the picot all around the outside edge of the brooch.

133

MATERIALS LIST

1 aurichalcite cabochon
approximately 4cm x 6cm

2 aurichalcite cabochons
approximately 12mm × 17mm

15 grams turquoise size 11°
seed beads (A)

20 grams turquoise silver-lined
size 11° seed beads (B)

2 grams turquoise silver-lined
size 14° seed beads (C)

174 turquoise 4mm bicone crystals (D)

174 clear 4mm bicone crystals (E)

74 turquoise/white 5.5mm
round glass beads (F)

19 teal crystal 6mm × 10mm briolettes (G)

2 grams size 8° clear seed beads (H)

10" (25cm) 2mm clear
rhinestone snake chain

½ sheet Lacy's StiffStuff™ backing material

6" (15cm) square white leather

1 pair glue-on post earring findings

6 lb. and 8 lb. crystal Fireline™

2 size 10 beading needles

1 size 10 sharps needle

Fabri-Tac™ Fabric Glue

Gem-Tac™ Permanent Adhesive

Blade scissors

Leather awl

Wire cutters

Bead sorting dish or cloth

aurichalcite necklace & earrings

The stones in this set are gorgeous examples of aurichalcite, a carbonate mineral mined near Magdelena, New Mexico. They were cut by Dean Crane of Two Cranes.

This necklace may look very complicated, but it is simply a combination of a number of the stitches presented in this book. It will take you awhile to make something this elaborate, but it is the kind of piece that will become an heirloom.

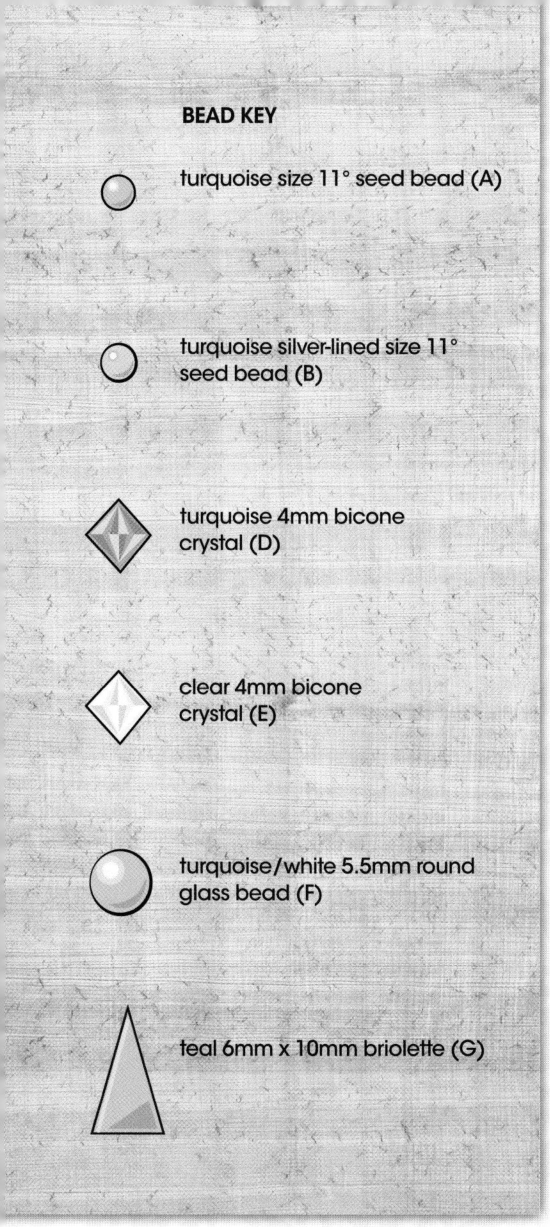

BEAD KEY

○ turquoise size 11° seed bead (A)

○ turquoise silver-lined size 11° seed bead (B)

◆ turquoise 4mm bicone crystal (D)

◇ clear 4mm bicone crystal (E)

○ turquoise/white 5.5mm round glass bead (F)

△ teal 6mm x 10mm briolette (G)

FIGURE 12–10

instructions

preparing the cabochons

1 Cut one 4" × 6" (10cm × 15cm) piece and two 2" (5cm) square pieces of StiffStuff™ backing.

2 Place a thin coat of gem glue on the backs of the cabochons. Glue each to a corresponding piece of backing. Let the glue dry thoroughly before proceeding.

beading the bezel on the pendant

1 Single-thread a needle with the 6lb. Fireline™ and knot the end.

2 Backstitch a ring of 11° turquoise seeds (A) around the cabochon as you did for the *Butterfly and Flowers Brooch* (pages 129–133).

3 Weave several rows of peyote stitch with the 11° turquoise seeds (A).

4 Halfway up the bezel, do a row of 11° turquoise silver-lined seeds (B).

5 Complete all but the last row with 11° turquoise seeds (A).

6 The final row in the bezel is done with 14° silver-lined turquoise beads (C). Pass through the last row again and pull as tightly as you can.

7 Pass down though the beads following the diagonal pattern to the underside. Tie off the thread.

adding the rhinestones

1. Bring a new strand of the 8lb. Fireline™ up from the underside, then thread on enough 8° clear seeds (H) to make a ring around the bezel.

2. Pass through the ring again to reinforce. Pass through to the underside and tack in place.

3. Couch the beads in place as you did for the *Butterfly & Flowers Brooch* (pages 129–133).

4. Lay the rhinestone chain over the ring of 8° clear seeds, checking for length. Do not trim at this point.

5. Beginning at 1 end of the chain, couch the chain into place *over* the ring of 8° clear seeds (H), using them as a base. You must do this so the rhinestones are high enough in the piece to be seen.

6. As you couch the chain into place, keep the rhinestones tightly together so as little connecting chain as possible shows.

7. When you get close to the end, trim off the excess chain with wire cutters; couch the remainder in place.

SIDE VIEW OF PENDANT

adding the turquoise/white beads

1. Starting with a new heavy thread, come up from the underside and string on enough 5.5mm turquoise/white round glass beads to make a ring around the rhinestones.

2. Pass through the ring again to reinforce.

3. Couch between every bead.

adding the turquoise seed beads

1. The next row of embellishment is a ring of the 11° turquoise seeds (A) you used to make the bezel.

2. Follow the steps in *Butterfly & Flowers Brooch* (pages 129–133) to couch the ring in place.

FIGURE 12–11

adding the turquoise and clear crystals

1 The final row of embellishment is a ring of alternating turquoise (D) and clear (E) 4mm bicone crystals.

2 Follow the steps in *Butterfly & Flowers Brooch* (pages 129–133) to couch the ring in place.

adding the fringe

1 When you have completed the final row of couched beads, carefully trim the excess backing material away from the beaded area, leaving about ¼" (6mm). You will trim closer just before your final step.

2 Determine how you wish the stone to hang on the necklace. There is no right or wrong, just personal preference. Also, some stones simply look better one way than another.

3 Decide where you wish to hang the fringe (this is optional—again, according to personal preference).

4 Bring a new thread out at the point where you wish to start the fringe, against and almost under the last row of beading.

5 Refer to the Bead Key (Figure 12–10, page 135) and to Figure 12–11. Using the abbreviations given in the Bead Key and *Materials List* (page 134), thread on 3 (B), 1 (E), 1 (A), 1 (D), 1 (A), 1 (E), 1 (B), 1 (F), 1 (B), 1 (D), 1 (A), 1 (E), 1 (A), 1 (D), 1(B), 1 (F), 3 (A), 1 (G) and 3 (A).

6 Pass the needle back trough the last *F* you picked up and all the remaining beads in the fringe above it.

7 Pass the needle into the fabric at the top, being sure to pull the thread through so the beads are snug and no thread shows.

8 Pass to the side about 1/8" (3mm) and repeat Steps 5–7 until you have made the width of fringe you want. An uneven number of fringes usually looks better (the sample has 19).

9 Tie off the thread, glue the knots and trim the excess threads.

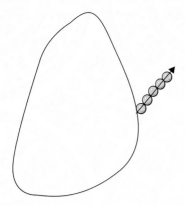

FIGURE 12–12

FIGURE 12–13

finishing the pendant

1 Cut a piece of leather just slightly larger than the beaded pendant.

2 Glue the leather to the back of the beaded pendant with the fabric glue. Allow to dry thoroughly.

3 Trim the excess backing and leather to 1/8" (3mm) around the edge of piece.

4 Cut a new piece of 8lb. Fireline™ and knot the very end.

5 Work the knot in between the backing and the leather somewhere under the fringe and bring the needle through the backing material to the front.

6 Refer to Figure 12–12. Pick up 5 turquoise silver-lined size 11° seeds (B) and do a whip stitch over the edge of the piece: Simply pass the needle from the front around to the back of the piece, and bring the needle up through to the front about a bead's width away from your 1st stitch (see Figure 12–13).

7 Repeat Step 6 around the entire piece until you get back to where you started. Note that as you do this stitch, the beads will look like they are at an angle to the edge of the piece. This is how they are supposed to look.

8 Set the piece aside while you make the neck strap.

WHEN SEWING LEATHER

Always bring the needle through the leather straight. Never try to push the needle through at an angle as it is much harder to pierce the leather that way. If you use a sharps needle and push it straight through, it should work easily.

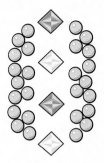

FIGURE 12–14

making the neck strap

1 Make the neck strap using the basic instructions from the *Right Angles & Ladders Bracelet* (pages 123–127). Follow the section on *Weaving the Crystal Band* (page 124) using alternating clear (E) and turquoise (D) crystals and the turquoise silver-lined size 11° seeds (B) as shown in Figure 12–14.

You may begin the neck strap attached to the pendant or do it separately, attaching both ends when you are done.

2 Follow the instructions for *Weaving in the Matte Beads* (page 125) using turquoise size 11° seeds (A).

3 The project sample has no closure; if you wish to make your piece the same way, be sure it has enough length to go over your head. The project sample is about 24" (732cm) long.

You can make a shorter neck strap instead and incorporate a clasp.

4 Sew the neck strap to the pendant where you please, attaching it under the couched beads and hiding the threads. Tie off securely.

making the earrings

1 Make a beaded bezel around the stone as you did for the pendant using turquoise size 11° seeds (A). Make the last row of turquoise silver-lined size 11° seeds (B).

2 Couch a row of alternating clear (E) and turquoise (D) crystals around the bezel.

3 Trim the backing ¼" (6mm) away from the beads.

4 Roughly trim the leather to fit the backing.

5 Poke a hole in the upper half of the leather with an awl.

6 Apply glue to the underside of the earring pad around the post. Insert the earring post through the hole in the leather, making sure the glue sits against the leather.

7 Glue the leather to the earring backing with fabric glue. Allow the glue to dry thoroughly.

8 Trim the backing and leather close to the couched crystals.

9 Do a whip stitch over the edge using 3 turquoise silver-lined size 11° seeds (B).

10 Repeat all steps for the 2nd earring.

resources

Beads and Supplies

Christopher Neal,
The World Round
1222 John St.
Kalamazoo, MI 49001
(269) 352-8934
www.theworldround.com

David Christensen
David Christensen Blown
Glass Beads
(40) 294-1440

Off Center Productions
4339 30th Ave. SE
Lacey, WA 98503
(360) 491-0110
www.offcenterproductions.com

Wild Things Beads
P. O. Box 1990
Penn Valley, CA 95946
(530) 743-1339 between 10AM
and 6PM
www.wildthingsbeads.com

Glues

Beacon Adhesives
124 Mac Questen Parkway South
Mount Vernon, NY 10550
(914) 699-3400
www.beacon1.com

Findings & Stringing Wires

Beadalon
Wire and Cable Specialties
205 Carter Drive
West Chester, PA 19382
(866) 423-2325
www.beadalon.com

Claspon-Claspoff
Division of Bead Need
5735 S. University Drive
Davie, FL 33328
(954) 880-0880
www.claspon-claspoff.com

Gemstone Cabochons
Designer Cabs (Wire Wrapping)
369 Guillian Dr.
Branson, MO 65616
(417) 230-3929 or (417) 334-8485
e-mail: designercabs@yahoo.com

Two Cranes
P. O. Box 116
Socorro, NM 87801
(505) 835-9225
www.2cranes.biz

Lamp-Worked Beads

Kathy Johnson
KJ Originals
648 SW 152nd
Burien, WA 98166-2213
(206) 242-2860
http://kjoriginals.com

Tanya A. McGuire
TAM Designs
4291 Dakota Ave. South
Huron, SD 57350
(605) 352-1488
www.tanyamcguire.com

Teresa Provine
(405) 921-7777
www.shop.pleasantmemories.us

Polymer Clay

Lynne Ann Schwarzenberg
River Poet Designs
63 Hubbell Ave.
Ansonia, CT 06401
Phone (203) 732-4003 or
(203) 305-0767
www.riverpoetdesign.com

about the author

Carole Rodgers began her second art career by designing cross stitch for magazine articles. Finding her talents to be in demand, she then expanded into numerous other needlework and crafts disciplines, including beading.

Carole soon found herself designing from one hundred fifty to two hundred original projects per year for magazines, books, kits and project sheets. She is the author/designer of *Beaded Jewelry with Found Objects* (Krause Publications, 2004) and *Beading Basics* (Krause Publications, 2006) as well as ninety-nine pattern leaflets and hundreds of magazine articles. She holds five patents for new product development.

Carole teaches beading and needlework classes and has also served as a consultant to manufacturers in the craft industry. She has been actively involved in promoting crafts, beading and needlework in professional organizations and on craft television programs.

Although well-trained in numerous media, Carole admits her first love is beading. She has yet to find a beading technique that she doesn't like and is always on the lookout for new ones she hasn't tried.

index

Build your beading knowledge and skill with these great titles!

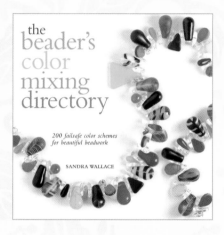

Beading Basics
Carole Rodgers

Build solid beading techniques with the detailed instructions, 35+ projects and more than 400 color photos and illustrations featured in this beginner's must-have.

Paperback, 128 pages, #BDGBS
ISBN-10: 0-89689-170-4
ISBN-13: 978-0-89689-170-8

The Beader's Bible
Dorothy Wood

This indispensable guide to beads and beading techniques presents essential beading know-how together with a wide range of inspirational projects, tips and ideas.

Paperback with flaps, 160 pages, #Z2314
ISBN-10: 0-7153-2300-8
ISBN-13: 978-0-7153-2300-7

The Beader's Color Mixing Directory
Sandra Wallace

Take your beadwork from mundane to magnificent using the basic color-mixing principles and step-by-step instructions featured in this must-have for every beginning beader. Each color scheme is illustrated on an item of jewelry.

Paperback, 128 pages, #Z0744
ISBN-10: 0-89689-480-0
ISBN-13: 978-0-89689-480-8